NINA WILLIS WALTER
LOS ANGELES CITY COLLEGE

Let Them Write Poetry

A book about the teaching of poetry appreciation
through the writing of poetry
For the teachers of children from kindergarten
through high school

HOLT, RINEHART AND WINSTON
New York · Chicago · San Francisco
Toronto · London

1234 090 98

Library of Congress Catalog Card Number: 62–11870
03–011385–7
Printed in the United States of America

Let Them Write Poetry

To My Grandchildren

PREFACE

Let Them Write Poetry is a handbook for teachers who are concerned with the development of the creative impulse in children and with the teaching of poetry appreciation through the writing of poetry. My basic assumptions are that true appreciation of any art is developed by experiences in the field of that art, and that poetry should be taught not objectively by dissection and analysis, but subjectively as a way of thought and a way of life.

My general purposes are to help the teacher encourage the creativeness of children, to suggest ways of making the reading and the writing of poetry a worthwhile experience for the individual and the group, and to help the teacher relate poetry to life situations.

My specific purposes are to help the teacher learn to tell the difference between creative and imitative work in poetry written by children, to present poetry to children in such a way as to call forth the poetic response to experience, to set up a workshop for practical experience with poetry, and to develop standards of evaluation for children's creative work in poetry.

Everything in this book has been tested by actual experience or has grown out of such experience. Every poem used as an illustration is the original work of the child whose name is under it, and it was written at the age indicated. Many of these poems were published in a little magazine that I edited from 1937 to 1943: *Nuggets, a Magazine of Poetry by Youth.* Others came out of classroom activities. Still others are the spontaneous expressions of today's children.

I hope that other teachers will have as much fun in using this book as I have had in putting it together.

Los Angeles
February 1962

N.W.W.

CONTENTS

Let Them Write Poetry

1 Awakening the Desire for Self-expression

POEM

When a poem
Is in my head,
It is like God talking
Just to me.
–Anita Ruiz, age 6

"POETRY LADY! WAIT!"

I had just parked my car in front of the elementary school in which I taught the sixth grade. A thin little girl about six years old was running down the sidewalk toward me. I recognized her as one of the first-graders in the class I visited frequently. She skidded to a stop in front of me.

"I have another poem in my head!" she exclaimed. "May I tell it to you?"

"Yes, indeed," I said. "I want to hear it."

I listened quietly while she recited the poem I have placed at the beginning of this chapter. Then, at her request, I wrote it on a piece of paper so that she could take it to her teacher. As I watched her skipping happily toward her classroom, with her skimpy little lunch sack in one hand and her precious poem clutched firmly in the other, I thought about her poem and her name for me and decided that I liked them both. Little Anita Ruiz was beginning to discover the pleasures of the imagination and the joy of self-expression.

In the process of trying to get children of all ages to put imagination to work and to express their own thoughts in their own words, I made a number of significant discoveries, which I shall summarize as briefly as I can. First of all, I discovered that the creative impulse in children is shy and is easily inhibited. It must be coaxed and encouraged. It cannot be coerced, and it should not be either disparaged or overpraised. The environment must be favorable for its development, and experiences must be provided for its encouragement. Because it is tied up so closely with the personality of the individual child, and because it takes so many different directions, in our classroom planning we must provide for variety and for freedom to experiment.

In order to get our pupils started in creative expression, we must do four things. First, we must provide a creative environment. Second, we must give our pupils creative experiences. Third, we must select sources of inspiration that will appeal to their imagination and start it functioning creatively. Fourth, we must give them a chance to write what they want to write, and we must *let them alone while they do it.*

CREATIVE ENVIRONMENT

Environment includes all of the objects, personalities, and influences with which the individual comes in contact. A creative environment in the classroom is one that challenges interest, thought, the desire to do something, and the urge to share with others the emotional experiences derived from successful activity. That urge to share is the foundation for creative expression, which may take any one of a number of forms. We are at present considering only one form of expression—creative poetry.

In the preparation of a proper environment for creative work, we must consider first of all the physical factors. These include classroom arrangement and decoration, materials for experiment, and provisions for freedom of movement. Anything we feature in our centers of interest—books, pictures, growing things, models, pets, children's prized collections—can be used to stimulate creative activity. Pictures, for example, can be made a vital part of the classroom environment. By relating the pictures we post to the unit of study and to the experience level of the child, and by changing them frequently, we provide a continuing stimulus for creative imagination. The effective use of newspaper clippings, magazine prints, travel folders, and especially original pictures by the children can make our centers of interest both interesting and inspiring. After the pictures have been removed from the bulletin board so that others may be posted, they should be filed in a large folder. The children should have access to this folder, so that they may continue to enjoy their favorite pictures. Poems and stories inspired by a particular picture may be attached to it or filed with it, so that the folder eventually becomes a class book.

Another important factor in the physical environment is the presence of a variety of materials for experiment, with sufficient freedom of movement to insure satisfactory results. The truly creative environment is one that is full of things to do and interesting materials with which to experiment. The classroom should be a children's room—of the children, by the children, for the children. A room so arranged provides the creative environment which is the first essential to the awakening of the creative impulse. Self-expression grows with the necessity of sharing exciting experiences with others.

Environment also includes certain intellectual factors, the most important of which are respect for originality, recognition of individual achievement, encouragement of self-expression, and flexible standards of value.

The world needs more originality. It needs people who are not afraid of new ideas, people who are willing to examine them, evaluate them, and apply them to the solution of our common problems. We cannot begin too young to inculcate in children a respect for originality. When they feel that we are sincere in our belief that their ideas, expressed in their own way, honestly, sincerely, imaginatively, are valuable, they will let us see something of their real thoughts and feelings. One goal of education is the growth and development of the individual into a self-respecting, well-balanced, socially useful citizen. The creative impulse plays an important part in such development. Therefore, we must be sure that the atmosphere of the classroom is one that will not discourage and inhibit the tentative gropings of the individual toward free and serious self-expression.

In order to get the child to be honest with himself, to attempt to express his own individuality, to respect his own ideas and give them a chance to grow, we must put the premium upon personal integrity and originality rather than upon clever imitations of approved patterns of thought. We must recognize individual achievement in self-expression and not compare one such expression unfavorably with another. Only in this way can we encourage those less expert with the tools of learning to continue to express their ideas. We must remember that standards of evaluation are flexible, that what shows progress in one case may not meet our expectations in another, that the important thing is not the production of finished poems but *individual growth.* We must remember that ideas are important, and we must treat ideas with respect.

Of equal importance with the physical and intellectual factors in environment is the emotional factor. Children need emotional security. They need to feel sure of sympathy and understanding. We shall never be able to awaken a child's intellectual pride in a real and serious creative effort if he senses that we are amused by what he has written or fears that we may read it to others for a laugh. Only when we have his complete confidence will he let us see into his heart, and we can gain that confidence only by taking seriously what he intends to be taken seriously, by refraining from attitudes of superiority, and by avoiding indifference or discouraging criticism.

Emotional security is not something that we can hand to a child at will. It is something that he must find for himself. Through the personal satisfaction that comes with the achievement of success, even if it is only the small success of finding the right words to express an idea, he learns to orient himself in a bewildering world and so moves forward toward that emotional security which his being craves. All that we can do is to point the way to the goal and stand by sympathetically, hopefully, while he stumbles toward it.

The emotional situation is perhaps the most subtle of all the environmental factors. One who is attempting to awaken the creative impulse and to obtain the creative response from children must be something of a psychologist as well as an opportunist. He must be able to detect unfavorable influences and change his plans at a moment's notice. He must realize that poetry cannot be made as a block of soap can be carved; it bubbles up from within as a result of a combination of favorable circumstances, inspiration, and preparation. The stage must be set for it.

There are certain classroom practices that will effectively obstruct creative effort, particularly in poetry. These are scolding, nagging, display of impatience by the teacher, threats of punishment for disorder, sarcastic remarks, and other disciplinary measures designed to keep the class in line. It is wise not to begin a period of creative poetry when the class is upset or when disorder threatens. For ideas come when the mood is right, when there is no friction, when friendliness and co-operation prevail, when there is no compulsion or restraint or antagonism in the air. We must choose our moments and be prepared to seize favorable opportunities for the advancement of creative writing.

CREATIVE EXPERIENCES

The creative impulse is the urge to give expression to an idea, an emotion, or an experience in beauty. It is the urge to make something, and it comes as a result of reflection about a creative experience. Back of the creative impulse lies the desire to share.

No child will be stirred to self-expression until he has had a creative experience to talk or write about, an experience which appeals to his imagination or makes an impression upon the sensitive plate of his emotions. Any experience is creative if it thrills him with a sudden recognition of beauty or with the perception of some truth which he has not noticed previously, if it arouses within him the feeling of discovery or the sense of participation in the realities of life, if it stirs his feelings or makes him think, if it leaves him with an urge to do something about it—to give artistic expression to his feelings and to share his ideas. Every experience of life has creative significance for the person who is mentally and emotionally awake.

In the primary grades experiences must be largely objective. Little children react to the things they can see and touch. In order to express his ideas of a tree, the child must look at a tree, observing the blend of browns, greens, and yellows, the interesting patterns of light and shadow, the shapes of the leaves, the way the bark grows. He must feel the bark and the leaves.

Creative experiences need not be complicated. Indeed, the simpler the experience, the more likely we are to get original expressions from primary children.

"Come into my room," a second-grade teacher invited me one day, "and help me get some poetry out of my pupils."

I entered the classroom carrying a large seashell which I had borrowed from a nature enthusiast. The children made a circle with their chairs, and together we began to speculate upon the former life of the shell. We ventured opinions as to where it came from, what had lived in it, and where it had been. Those who had been to the seashore told about shells they had found. We looked carefully at the shell and tried to think what it resembled. Then I held it up to my ear and listened intently.

"It's singing a song," I said. "Would you like to listen?"

Of course they would.

"See if you can tell me what the shell is singing," I invited, passing the shell to the nearest child. "Everybody will have a turn to listen. As soon as you know what the shell says, come and tell me."

I waited, pencil and paper ready.

"It doesn't sound like singing to me," the first little boy objected.

"Tell me what it sounds like to you," I urged.

"A bumblebee."

"Can you make a little story about it?"

The child thought for a moment. Finally his story came. I wrote it upon my paper and added his name and age.

"Write my story," the next one clamored. "It sounds like a bee to me, too. Buzz, buzz, buzz."

"But Johnny told that story," I pointed out. "I have already written it. See if you can think of another one."

A little girl came up and whispered to me. Several others followed her example. Soon they were waiting in line, each with a story to tell. Their teacher began to help with the writing. Several hurried back to have another turn at listening to the shell, so that they could tell another story. Obviously, they enjoyed the individual attention and the implication that their ideas were important. Expanding confidence was very noticeable.

"I want to hold my story, please," one little girl begged, as I finished writing what she had whispered to me.

"Me too, me too!" came a chorus of voices.

None of them could read their stories, but how proudly they showed one another "my story." Of course, not all of the stories were good. Most of them were complete sentences, which the teacher used in subsequent reading experiences. Many of them showed the stirring of imagination. A few were real poems. Not all of the children contributed, but we did not worry the unresponsive child and make him lose confidence in himself. Every child must not be expected to have a thought ready for each experience; for experiences which appeal to some children will not appeal to others. For this reason we must provide a variety of experiences.

The seashell has been used many times with children of different ages. The following bits of verse show the variety of thought that may come from the same experience. No two children will hear exactly the same sound or will be reminded of exactly the same thing.

THE SHELL SINGS

The seashell
Sings about the wind
Blowing hard
And pushing the water along.
–Patricia Monroe, age 7

SOUND OF A SEASHELL

The shell
Sounds like an airplane
Going over the sea,
Bumpity, bumpity, bump.
–Louis Kelly, age 8

SOUND OF THE SHELL

When I put the shell up to my ear,
It sounds like somebody praying
And singing in there.
–William Sanders, age 8

COWRIES

Cowries are very beautiful,
Cowries are very gay.
The song they sing so sweetly,
The song they sing today,
Sounds as if it were a roar
Coming from a music store.
—Josephine Caracho, age 12

THE COWRIE

The cowrie sings a song
Like a waterfall
Which runs all day long.
The flowers and trees
Cannot equal its beauty,
And the birds and bees
Cannot equal its song.
—Roy Tahajian, age 13

SONG OF THE COWRIE

The shell's song is like the wind
Roaring with all its might.
It makes me think of ice and snow
And a winter night.
—Rose Sukiasian, age 13

Almost any primary activity can serve as the basis for the exercise of creative imagination. Flowers brought to school by a child may be examined closely, and children may be asked to tell of what they are reminded when they look at the flowers. This exercise introduces them to simple imagery. Pets, things made by the children in the schoolroom, excursions, and simple aspects of nature can be subjected to observation and discussion with the purpose of stimulating imaginative expression.

Creation in the primary grades is largely the unconscious expression of the child's immediate, unreflecting reaction to objects.

Emotional experiences play very little part in creative expression at this age level. The child's creative experiences must come from his own activities or from a deliberately awakened consciousness of some concrete manifestation of nature.

One teacher allowed her first-graders time to watch the rain, to listen to it, to talk about what it does. Another had everybody else in school watching for a rainbow so that she could hurry her class out to see it. Afterwards, the children talked about it, drew pictures of it, and told stories about it. Each child was encouraged to tell what the rainbow looked like or made him think of. Other teachers have encouraged their pupils to feel the beauty of the rainbow and to make it a part of their consciousness by trying to reproduce the form and the colors with crayons or paint, by trying to make word pictures of it, by trying to express its significance in terms of their own personalities. The rainbow was a creative experience to the children who made the following poems:

GOD'S RAINBOW

Rain and sun
Make a rainbow
For God.
–Earl Lamothe, age 7

A RAINBOW

Oh what a lovely day,
When the clouds all cry.
Then a rainbow bursts forth
Like neon lights in the sky.
The clouds drift away
Like beautiful fairies on high.
–Patricia Evelyn Ball, age 9

THE RAINBOW

Sometimes in the gray sky
I look above
And see a rainbow curve.
It shines like a candy hill
Against the clouds.
–Woodson Henry, age 8

FAIRY CIRCLE

The rainbow looks like a fairy circle
    Away up in the sky.
Don't you think that the fairies
    Are walking on it by sly?
        –Marjorie Slaughter, age 10

RAINBOW

The rainbow
Looks like a bridge
That the moon floats over,
Or like the sun
Over the ocean
When it goes down.
    –Cleo Baker, age 12

AFTER THE RAIN

After the rain is over,
And the sky is blue and clear,
You will know that someone has done her up
In a beautiful ribbon, for cheer.

The sun spreads his rays upon it;
But the trails of colors fade.
For if the sky had to wear it forever,
We'd forget how her ribbon was made.
    –Sadie Baldonado, age 14

Reading and observation, as well as contact with things, can provide creative experiences for older children. Remembered experiences, imagined experiences, ideas about the natural world, and emotional experiences are creative experiences when the child's attention is directed toward discovering what they mean to him personally and toward putting his thoughts and feelings about them into imaginative and artistic form. A teacher can provide creative experiences by giving the children an opportunity to read, hear, and discuss poetry which will awaken in them an appreciation of words and word pictures; by showing them where to look for beauty and for significance in their surroundings; by allowing them to experiment with arts and crafts materials; by showing them how to use in their own lives the results of school activities; by allowing them to assume and carry out on their own responsibility some service designed to improve the group situation; by planning first-hand participation in community activities.

SOURCES OF INSPIRATION

Back of all creative work there must be inspiration of some sort. Inspiration is the pinprick that starts the creative impulse functioning. The main purpose of the creative experiences we plan for our classes is to provide the inspiration necessary for successful expression. But if, in our search for sources of inspiration, we ourselves remain uninspired, the results of our creative writing periods are likely to be disappointing. Therefore, we should, first of all, consider sources of inspiration for the teacher. Most of us seek so-called cultural experiences for our own personal satisfaction, but few of us try to put any of that satisfaction into words. We do not consciously try to express just what a concert, a play, a picture, or a sunset has meant to us as individuals; hence, we miss the deepest thrill of all, the thrill that comes from the interpretation of an experience in terms of beauty or significance.

At a meeting of my class in creative writing for teachers, which I taught for Los Angeles State College, I made a little speech, as follows:

"If you would awaken in children an awareness of significant details and of bits of beauty in their environment, you must be aware of those things yourself. Intellectual apprehension is not enough; you must *feel* that beauty, and you must be able to express your feeling in terms that will make children feel it, too. Plan for the deepening and expansion of your own impressions by consciously exercising the creative faculty. Imagination needs as much exercise as muscles need."

"How?" asked a young teacher. "I never wrote a poem in my life. I don't think I can."

"I'm afraid some of us were long ago conditioned against the writing of poetry," said another. "The very idea frightens us."

"Don't think of it as *writing a poem,*" I suggested. "Think of it as exercising imagination. Try to make a single image about a thing by asking yourself what it looks like or sounds like *to you*. Don't let yourself fall into the habit of remembering other people's images for common experiences; create your own."

"That is not as easy as it sounds," a third teacher remarked. "While I am driving to school, I try to make images, but sometimes I drive for many blocks before my eye alights upon something that triggers my imagination."

"Keep practicing," I advised. "The first images come hard—and I hope you remember that when you ask your class to make them. But after a while you will not need to search the whole horizon for something worthy of an image. When you find the images coming easily, try your skill on commonplace things. Keep a little notebook and jot down images that occur to you. It will be a means of checking your progress in the expansion of imagination, and some of those images will come in handy later. Sometimes just the effort of thinking about a thing, of trying to express it in terms of imagery, will open up a whole new train of thought. After a little practice of this sort, you will find it easy to spot the significant things in the schoolroom environment, and easy to lead the children to see the beauty in common things. You will not need, then, to search for sources of inspiration; you will need only to select."

"I certainly hope so," sighed the young teacher who had started the discussion. "But couldn't we list some sources of inspiration now, so that I'll know where to look?"

The following outline is the result of that request. It is intended only as a reminder of the great variety of experiences which can inspire children to creative self-expression.

SOURCES OF INSPIRATION

I. In the schoolroom
- A. Activities, games, stories, music
- B. Creative work in other fields
- C. Objects: vases, bowls, models, toys, artifacts
- D. Pictures

- E. Living things: flowers, plants, insects, pets
- F. Exhibits
- G. Things seen from the windows

II. The out-of-doors
- A. Trees, flowers, plants, gardens, growing things
- B. Animals, insects, birds
- C. Mountains, rivers, lakes, oceans
- D. Stars, sun, moon, clouds, sky
- E. Seasons, night, day, sunrise, sunset
- F. Wind, storms, rain, fog, thunder, lightning
- G. Playtime activities

III. Relations with people
- A. Parents and other adults
- B. Brothers and sisters
- C. Friends
- D. Neighbors
- E. Babies

IV. Special occasions: holidays, excursions, and the like

V. The city
- A. Buildings: tall buildings, old buildings, new buildings, memorials, and others
- B. Bridges
- C. Industrial activities, machines, men at work
- D. Street noises
- E. Transportation facilities
- F. Parks
- G. Other centers of interest

VI. The country
- A. Farms, farmers, farm activities
- B. Fields, crops, orchards
- C. Farm animals
- D. Woods, forests, streams
- E. Roads, lanes, paths, fences, gates

VII. Personal experiences
- A. Immediate experiences
- B. Remembered experiences
- C. Imagined experiences

VIII. Books

IX. Poetry
- A. Read aloud by the teacher or others
- B. Read silently
- C. Creative work of other children
- D. Bulletin-board displays

AWAKENING THE CREATIVE IMPULSE

We have provided a creative environment in the classroom and many creative experiences. From the numerous sources of inspiration we have selected those which seem most likely to appeal to the class. But before the class begins to write poetry, there is one other thing we must do: we must awaken the creative impulse. We must help the children to realize that passive acceptance of an experience is not enough; we must teach them to make the imaginative, artistic response to the experience.

Naturally, children do not come ready-made with all of the impulses and modes of self-expression that we adults have acquired. Many of them have been inhibited from infancy; they do not realize the nature of the force that gets them into difficulties and drives them to do unaccountable things. It is our job to help them learn to make constructive use of that force; if we wish them to use a part of it in creative self-expression, we must show them that self-expression is possible, is desirable, is fun.

The approach may be made in various ways, depending upon the age and maturity of the group. The inventiveness of primary children can be aroused to discover simple and delightful analogies by playing the game "What is it like?" "A tree is like a giant," says one. "It is like a fan," says another. "A tent," says a third. Whatever the analogy, imagination has been awakened to perceive the ways in which common objects can remind us of other things. Very small children can find pictures in clouds, can see the ants in the grass as little people in a tall green forest, can think what a doll would say if it could talk. With a little encouragement they soon get into the spirit of the game and speak freely about any activity, experience, or observation. But they should be wholly unconscious of effort to do anything with *words*. They should not be told that they are making poetry, or that they must try to think of special words so that what they say will be poetry, lest they become self-conscious and their expressions become stilted. It is the natural child that we want, expressing himself in a natural way about an experience.

The teacher, however, must be on the alert to catch and record unobtrusively any expressions that are refreshingly original, apt, or imaginative. Long-sustained poetic expressions must not be expected. The beginner's poetry will be short. Any urging to add to the thought will disrupt the unity and give it artificiality and will tend to discourage creativeness.

With children in the intermediate grades the technique is somewhat different. Most of them will be able to write their own thoughts. Class discussion of an experience, with an invitation to make images or help with a group response in poetic form, will often arouse interest and start imagination to work. Children at this age level may be taught to think of their little verses as word pictures, may consciously try to make word pictures that would help an artist in making a painting. They may be taught the simile—the form, rather than the term. They may make a game of it. To how many things can they liken a passing airplane? "What does it look like to you?" may be asked. Or, "What does it sound like?" Or, "What does it make you think of?" After a few such games they will learn to ask themselves such questions when they tell or write about an experience, and to incorporate the answers in their poems. The game helps to develop in them a feeling for color, sound, and other sensory appeals, as well as attentiveness to small and interesting details.

The same questions may be used in the upper grades, with the addition of "How does it make me feel?" The creative impulse can best be awakened in older children by practice with some of the materials of creation and a study of the results. They should have repeated opportunities to read and hear and discuss beautiful poetry which is within their range of understanding, especially poems that other children have written. A child gains in confidence and initiative if he knows that he is not being expected to do more than is done by other children of his age. We may start the creative impulse functioning by showing the children where to look for beauty, how to use and develop their imaginations, and how to put the results on paper; by helping them to find the right words—beautiful, significant, splendid words; by calling attention to words and word patterns of unusual beauty and power in their reading materials. We should make the effort worth while by preserving their work in some form as an incentive to add to their collection and to watch their own improvement in word choice and usage.

A more direct approach may be made to junior- and senior-high-school students. Most of them have learned that poetry is a part of their cultural heritage, and they expect some of their work to be with poetry. We might begin with a preliminary talk somewhat as follows, or a discussion that would bring out these points:

> Why do we write poetry? We write poetry for the same reason that an artist paints or a musician composes—for the personal satisfaction that we get from creative effort. We write because some inner force impels us to try to give verbal expression to what has touched us deeply. We write to satisfy an urge to share an experience in beauty. And we write poetry because it is fun. It is fun to make words serve as brushes to paint our pictures, to discover new meanings in common words, and to find the exact words in which to express an idea. It is fun to watch our vocabularies grow, to feel ourselves coming to a better understanding of life as we let our minds linger about an experience in the search for words in which to express its significance. The successful re-creation of an emotional experience in terms of poetry produces the personal satisfaction that goes with all creative work and makes us happy in the activity.

"What do I do next?" asked one of my teacher-students with an eighth-grade class.

"Show them one or two simple things about poetry," I suggested. "Read aloud a few short poems, and allow them to select the images and the picture words. Almost anything you can find in *Early Moon,* by Carl Sandburg, or *The Dreamkeeper,* by Langston Hughes, will lend itself to this exercise. Other collections especially helpful at the junior-high-school level are the anthologies edited by Mrs. Waldo Richards: *High Tide, Magic Carpet,* and *Star Points.* Search your school library for collections and anthologies containing poems that appeal to teen-agers."

"Don't you think hearing poems by experts might discourage them from writing their own?" someone ventured.

"Yes, if you insist on a finished poem as the assignment," I replied. "But don't ask for the finished poem. Ask for a sentence containing an image, or a paragraph containing picture words. Invite them to write poetry if they feel so inclined, but do not insist upon it, for the older child is usually more skeptical than the primary child, more inhibited, and more doubtful of his ability to create. Also, his gregarious instinct makes him suspicious of anything that sets him apart from the herd, and therefore he will be somewhat slower to respond to the invitation to express himself poetically. It may be that you will need to convince your group that their ideas are really important and are worth recording."

"How? What shall I *say?*"

This question has been asked of me many times. Into the following paragraph I have packed the ideas that I try to promote in any class in which I try to develop creative expression. I have used them as introductory remarks for a creative writing project. I sincerely believe these things to be true, and I try to help each individual child to feel that his own original ideas are important. I suspect that it is the sincerity of my approach, rather than my exact words, that inspires creative activity. I may say all this, or I may mimeograph the paragraph and put it into the hands of the students; but unless my *attitude* shows that I respect them and their work, nothing happens. Here is the paragraph:

> Your ideas are important. Certainly they are important, because they are *you* trying to peck through the shell that everybody thinks is you. When you have an idea all your own, don't be afraid of it because it is new and different and perhaps startling. Bring it out into the light, examine it, evaluate it, acknowledge it, and be proud of it. Encourage your imagination to work freely and your mind to speak freely through your writing. When you write a poem, don't be content with a weak imitation of another poet's meter and manner. Develop your own. Your ideas, expressed in your own way, honestly, sincerely, imaginatively, are worth just as much as the ideas of the greatest poet that ever lived.

Another approach to creative writing is the workshop method. The children may be given copies of a short easy poem containing an image, a poem such as this one:

STARS

The *stars are* God's *lanterns*
  Lighting His way
Each night after darkness
  Closes the day.
    –Lee Winters, age 13

First, they should underline the image, as indicated by italics. Then they should try to make other images about the stars. The images need not be worked out as poems; single phrases will do. The children may be allowed to read their images to the class and select the best phrases. This method acts as a stimulus for original work and is especially useful with immature or slow groups.

Once the creative impulse has been awakened and has started to function, the interest in creative writing is bound to grow, especially if the teacher is really interested and enthusiastic. Children always respond to sincerity. The teacher might begin by presenting a program of readings on poetry and poetry writing. In the appendix to this book I have listed some helpful books in three categories, as follows: (1) books about poetry, (2) poetry for children and young people, (3) poetry by children. I suggest that books of poetry be kept on the browsing table and that children be encouraged to share with the class their own books of poetry and their favorite poems.

2 The Teaching of Poetry

DEDICATION

I dedicate this book
To my English teacher,
Who taught me
What poetry is,
Who gave me time
To write these poems,
Who never laughed
At my fumblings,
Who saw the tiny flakes of gold
In my ton of ore
And helped me pan them.
–Olin Sanders, age 16

WHAT COULD BE A BETTER PRINT-shop project than a little book of one's own verse? And what a rewarding experience for the teacher who discovered a budding talent and, through two semesters, watched it grow.

One part of our task in the teaching of poetry is the development of the appreciation of poetry as an art form and as an expression of a poet's attitudes and reactions to experience. We must give our students a chance to get used to the manner and mood of poetry so that they will develop a real appreciation and understanding of the emotional and intellectual values involved in the writing of poetry.

DEVELOPING APPRECIATION

Generally speaking, the term "appreciation" is used rather vaguely to mean liking or enjoyment. But in order to determine its value as a goal in education, we must look beyond the simple denotation to a deeper significance.

The dictionary defines appreciation first as "the just valuation or proper estimate of worth or merit." Unfortunately, educators for years have been inclined to accept that definition and to evaluate poetry by dissecting it, by approaching it from an intellectual point of view, in order to form a "proper estimate of its worth or merit." However, we are coming to understand that whatever is rooted in emotion does not lend itself successfully to rigid intellectual classification.

The second part of the dictionary definition defines appreciation as a "rise in value." This is the part which should give us pause. For it is only when poetry comes to have a deep personal significance to him that the individual truly appreciates it. It rises in value to him as he feels its effect upon his emotional processes. When something affects pleasurably the emotional processes of the individual, he makes a favorable response to it, an active personal response. His feeling and his understanding become integrated, and his insights deepen.

Frequently, poetry as taught in school arouses no response other than an attempt on the part of conscientious students to memorize a few facts about it in case of a test. It is probable that lack of response on the part of the students is a reflection of the teacher's lack of response to the poem. No one can dissect and destroy the beauty of a poem that really means something to him personally. No teacher should attempt to present to students for appreciation a poem that leaves him cold. The teacher who never is personally stirred by any poem should do something about it. Perhaps he has never given poetry an opportunity to mean anything other than something to be taught.

Because appreciation is an active favorable response, it can not be developed in one who only sits and listens. Nor can it be aroused by the teacher who, in trying to avoid the pedagogical approach, goes to the other extreme and raves about the poems. Unless they are moved by the emotion in the poem itself, children will probably be stolidly unmoved, if not actively antagonized, by the emotion of the teacher presenting it. They are quick to sense insincerity.

In the development of appreciation we should begin with the known and proceed cautiously to the unknown. The following directives suggest helpful activities:

1. Begin with the poems that the children already know and love. Read them aloud.
2. Teach the children to read poems aloud, individually and in chorus.
3. Allow *those who wish to do so* to memorize their favorite poems. Do not make arbitrary assignments of memory work on poems that you want children to appreciate.
4. Encourage the class to select poems for reading aloud and to clip from newspapers and magazines poems which they enjoy.
5. Allow the class to collect and copy into a special class book poems that are closely related to the unit of study. Let the artists in the class illustrate them.
6. Encourage children to illustrate their own poems.
7. Allow children to find poems to go with favorite pictures or pictures to go with favorite poems.
8. Use a bulletin board as a center of interest devoted to poetry.

These activities tend to awaken interest in the poem as an art form and in the complete poem as the artistic expression of the poet's idea.

The next step is the discussion of specific poems. We ask ourselves these questions:

1. Why do we like some poems better than others?
2. Why do we remember some poems better than others?
3. Why do we remember some poems longer than others?
4. In a particular poem what idea is the poet trying to express?
5. What images make the poem stand out in our memory and help the poet to express his idea?
6. How do the rhythm and the pattern help us to enjoy the poem?

In short, we try to find out something of the why and the how of poetry by examining the different ways in which poets present their ideas.

As a result of the careful examination of individual poems appealing to children, we find that two qualities stand out: (1) a picturesqueness based upon imagery that makes a definite, unforgettable impression upon the mind; (2) an experience which is shared or can be shared by the reader. We teach the children to listen for the images, the picture words, the common experiences. We read to them poetry of all sorts until they learn to listen to it with understanding, until they begin to read poetry for themselves, voluntarily and with enjoyment. When we find them choosing books of poetry for their free-reading period, or pausing over the poems in other books, we know that the objective has been attained, that they have arrived at a real appreciation of poetry.

STIMULATING THE CREATIVE RESPONSE

Students who are merely studying poetry may choose anything that has appeal to the particular age level, and they may occasionally touch upon the more mature ideas as conditions seem right for them. But when the objective is to obtain a definite creative response in the form of original poetry, certain principles of selection should be observed.

The first of these principles is brevity. The original expressions of young children are nearly always brief, as are those of the beginner in poetry at any age level. Children who write long rambling verses are usually imitating what they have read. The very young child is rarely capable of the sustained emotion essential to the production of a long poem. He may respond to prodding by adding lines to his poems, but usually the added lines sound forced, are inferior to the original thought, and break the unity of the poem. In such productions the heavy hand of the teacher is clearly evident. Since our goal is the natural child expressing himself in a spontaneous, natural way, we must let him say as much as he will about his subject and accept what he has to say. If he stops short of completion, we must remember that he himself is immature. Perhaps he has caught just a hazy glimpse of something beyond his comprehension. That glimpse is all he should express at the moment, and we should not put pressure on him to exceed his capabilities for the sake of a finished poem.

Because the child's own poem will be brief, brevity should

characterize the poems presented to him for the purpose of stimulating the creative impulse. He should be allowed to see that brevity is an advantage rather than a detriment to the successful expression of ideas. If he is introduced to only long complicated poems, he will think disparagingly of his own brief bits, and he may become discouraged and refuse to try to write. We should make use of the many excellent poems which are short, simple, and colorful, and therefore have inspirational value for children.

The second principle of selection is simplicity of idea. Children respond most quickly and wholeheartedly to those poems which do not need to be analyzed, dissected, and explained. Furthermore, since a child cannot make either an emotional or an intellectual response to aspects of life which are too mature for his understanding or experience, we must not present poems that are beyond him in these respects.

Simplicity of phrasing and diction are also essential. The meanings of words and phrases should be immediately apparent to the children. The great poems, the difficult poems, the poems which arouse them to thought rather than to action, should be saved for poetry-appreciation lessons. Since the vocabulary of children's original work will be limited by the age and grade level of the group, the vocabulary of poems read to them for inspiration should be appropriate to the age and grade level.

The younger the child, the more definite and concrete should be the imagery. Children are most impressed by the poem which paints a clear picture with striking images and picture words. Since we are going to begin the actual writing of poetry by teaching them to use their imaginations to produce images, the poems we use for inspirational purposes should illustrate the process of expressing ideas in images.

Furthermore, we must choose poems that present experiences children will recognize with pleasure. It is not enough that the poems have the universality that is recognized as one of the essential qualities of all true poetry; they must have the universality of childhood. They must present experiences that are shared or can be shared by the young listeners.

Finally, we must select poems that have simplicity of pattern. The more complicated forms may be reserved for lessons in poetry appreciation. We are trying to get children to express their intimate thoughts and feelings naturally; therefore, we must not hamper them by holding them to patterns and forms which will cause them to speak self-consciously, artificially, or with restraint. We are working not for a finished poem, but for individual growth. We allow children to see by example that poetry need not rhyme, that line lengths need not be all the same, and we use the modern things, the free-verse bits that will demonstrate the freedom of expression we are trying to encourage.

To summarize: the poetry which will best stimulate the creative response is poetry which is short; which has simplicity of idea, of phrasing, of diction; which uses imagery; which is emotionally and intellectually suited to the age level; which presents experiences common to childhood; which is written in free verse or in simple rhythms.

PRESENTING POETRY EFFECTIVELY

In order to teach poetry creatively, we must make of every poem a creative experience. Have we done our duty by poetry when we solemnly read a poem aloud and say, "Isn't that beautiful, children?" Just what do we mean when we say "beautiful"? What is there in the poem that merits discussion? What has the poem to give to us, and how can we make it "give"?

Children should be prepared for a poem, especially if the poem presents new words or a new point of view. They should be asked to listen for specific things, as the poem is read, and should learn the delight of discovery. In that way they will learn how a poem is made and perhaps will understand why the particular poem was made. Children are not allowed to make scientific discoveries for themselves without some preparation for their experiments, nor should they be allowed to enter the mazes of poetry without some guideposts to assist them in orienting themselves.

Each poem that is read to a class should re-create, as much as possible, the setting, the mood, and the emotion which induced the poet to produce it. By the reading of the poem, by the remarks that we make about it, and by the things we emphasize we help the children to enter into and share the experience of the poet and thus to appreciate the poem.

The approach will necessarily be different for each poem. We should determine beforehand just what will be the most effective approach for each. We should familiarize ourselves with each poem that we intend to read. And then we should learn to read it naturally and effectively. One of the commonest reasons for lack of success with a poetry lesson is the teacher's inability to read the poems well.

Very young children may be asked to listen for one special thing in each poem. In one poem they may listen for colors; in another, for words that tell or imitate sounds; in another, for words that sound alike. They may be asked to find out where the poet was or what he was seeing or what he was thinking. When a poem lends itself to dramatization, children may volunteer to act out what the poet says.

Older children, also, need a little help in visualizing poetry. They need to listen for colors, for sound values, for words that describe the setting or suggest the mood, for rhymes, for characteristic rhythms. For example, Josephine Burr's "Night at Sea"[1] is a lovely poem, but it has unfamiliar words and an emotional connotation which may be lost upon children if the only method of presentation is reading aloud without comment.

The following directives may be helpful to the teacher who is nervous about presenting poetry to a class:

1. Read aloud poems containing images, and ask the class to listen for and record the images. Poems suggested:
   "Glimpse in Autumn" by Jean Starr Untermeyer
   "Dandelion" by Hilda Conkling
   "Moon Poems" by Vachel Lindsay
   "The Grasshopper" by Vachel Lindsay
   "Theology" by Joyce Kilmer
   "Chimes" by Alice Meynell
   "A Tree at Dusk" by Winifred Welles
   "Silver" by Walter de la Mare
   "White Nocturne" by Conrad Aiken
   "Symphony in Yellow" by Oscar Wilde
   "The Fog" by Carl Sandburg
2. Study each poem until you can read it aloud and can fit tone and emphasis to the swift emotional variations.

[1] Mrs. Waldo Richards, *Magic Carpet*. Boston: Houghton Mifflin Company, 1924.

3. Interpret the mood and the emotion with your voice, as a pianist interprets a musical composition with his fingers.
4. As you read, watch your class. Some children will respond immediately to your voice; others—those who need orientation—will be unimpressed.
5. Set a specific problem for each poem. For example, in a poem of action emphasize the discovery of action words. Read the poem a second time, line by line, examining each phrase for action words, and get definitions of words that may be unfamiliar. Show how the action builds up and then dies down. Then read the poem again, as a whole, without comment, and watch the class rise to it. Poems suggested:

   "Lochinvar" by Sir Walter Scott
   "The Highwayman" by Alfred Noyes
   "Paul Revere's Ride" by Henry Wadsworth Longfellow
   "Barbara Frietchie" by John Greenleaf Whittier
   "Casey at the Bat" by Ernest Lawrence Thayer

6. In presenting John Gould Fletcher's "Night of Stars,"[2] mention briefly what the Imagists stood for in poetry, and let the class determine as you read how the poem illustrates Imagist theory. After the first reading for total impression, ask the class to listen for new ways of saying things about the stars. Count and list on the blackboard the ways in which the poet has said, "The sky is bright with stars." Ask the class to think of other ways of expressing the same thought. Show them that one poem may help us to build another by setting us to thinking.
7. Robert Hillyer's poem "A Gull"[3] contains a symbol. Develop the meaning of the word "symbol." Ask the class to try to discover the symbol as you read. What question does the poet ask himself? When he was writing this poem, was he thinking only of the gull? Does his setting match his symbol?
8. Read "The Searchlight"[4] by Daniel Henderson. Discuss the meanings of unfamiliar words briefly, but do not drag out the discussion until the children become bored. The important thing is not vocabulary drill, but an appreciation of the poem and an understanding of the poet's meaning. Talk about the searchlight, and let the children tell what a searchlight at night makes them think of. List a few of the

[2] *Ibid.* [3] *Ibid.* [4] *Ibid.*

images on the blackboard. What did Mr. Henderson think the searchlight resembled?

9. "Sea Fever"[5] by John Masefield is a favorite poem with adolescents. Ask the class to explain what the poet was thinking about when he wrote this poem. Notice the excellent use of picture words, and the way in which each one helps to clarify the picture. Picture words include not only things seen, but also things heard and felt. Help the class to discover these qualities, which have made "Sea Fever" outstanding: the vivid picturesqueness of the language; the rhythm, which suggests the rhythm of the sea or of a ship on the sea; the imagery; the emotional quality; the simplicity.
10. Do not fall into the old method of classification and analysis. It does not matter if a child fails to understand every word in the poem or if all the poet's intentions are not clear to him. Call attention very briefly to a few things that you think will help him to understand a poem, and do not let the proceedings drag. Do not treat the poem as if the child will never have a chance to read it again and discover new meanings for himself. Focus his attention on significant details so that he will begin to understand why the poet wrote the poem and how he wrote it, and will be moved by some of the same feeling that moved the poet to write as he did.

USING IMAGINATION

In the teaching of poetry, imagination is both an objective and a criterion. It is an objective when we teach poetry in order to awaken imagination and to start it functioning creatively. It is a criterion when we use it as a measuring stick. For imagination is the quality that distinguishes poetry from mere verse.

Unfortunately, much of what passes for poetry by children is just verse, and not poetry at all, because the verse is based upon observation only. It is not the ability to see things that makes the poet, but the ability to see in them analogies and implications and significances hitherto unthought of by the casual observer. Observation *only* is just observation, and as such has its place in the scheme of education, but not as poetry. It is the basis of poetry, the caterpillar on

[5] *Ibid.*

the leaf of reality. Imagination is necessary to transmute it into the butterfly. Without imagination a poem never takes wings.

What is imagination? It is not the picture-taking quality of the eye, as many embryo poets seem to believe, but the picture-forming power of the mind. It is the quality that helps us to see the rainbow in a muddy pool, pictures in clouds, wings on a caterpillar. It enables us to see in common things some transcendent quality that lifts them above the ordinary, some likeness to things totally different, some hidden beauty revealed only to the sympathetic eye. It helps us to share our experiences with other people.

How are we to get children to use imagination in their writing? It is not sufficient to say to them, "Use your imagination." We might get the answer that came from one earnest little girl: "I would, teacher, but I can't find it anywhere." We must explain to children in terms that they can understand, and play games with them until they recognize the quality in their own work and in the work of others. We must be sure that we ourselves know the difference between observation and imagination. The following chart may be helpful in making that difference clear.

OBSERVATION	IMAGINATION
What a doll looks like.	What a doll thinks about; what it would say if it could talk.
Description of a tree in terms of shape or color.	Description of a tree by analogy, using simile or metaphor.
Description of a soap bubble in terms of size, shape, and color.	Description of a soap bubble in terms of analogy, by likening it to something else.
Description of clouds in terms of size, shape, or color.	Seeing pictures in clouds, or using clouds as images for something else.
Telling what a rabbit looks like in the snow.	Thinking how the rabbit might feel in the snow.
Describing appearances.	Finding meaning behind appearances.
Telling how music sounds.	Telling what music reminds us of, or what thoughts come to us when we hear music.
Taking pictures with our eyes.	Making pictures in our minds.

Examples

The clouds are white and the sky is blue.	The clouds are white lilies in a blue vase.
The butterfly is black and yellow.	The butterfly is a floating flower.
The rainbow has pretty colors.	The rainbow is the fairies' bridge.
The pepper tree is large and green.	The pepper tree is dressed in a green-lace hoop skirt.
The jet plane leaves a vapor trail in the sky.	A giant snail has crawled across the sky.
The sunset is red.	The sunset burns the western sky with long tongues of flame.

I find that even young children can understand the difference between observation and imagination if I give them concrete examples such as the following:

> Suppose you look out the window and say, "Oh, I see a butterfly!" Have you used imagination? Not if the butterfly is really there. Suppose you say, "I see a pretty yellow butterfly on the purple flowers." Have you used imagination? Not yet. The butterfly is there and the flowers are there, and they really are a butterfly and flowers. But suppose you think about the butterfly for a while and then say, "The butterfly is a fairy's golden airplane sailing over the purple flowers." Have you used imagination? Yes, because you have been able to see how an ordinary object is like something very different. Your statement has gone through three stages. The first stage is obviously not poetry. The second stage makes the picture come alive by the addition of color words and is often mistaken for poetry. But it is still just a picture. The third stage satisfies the first qualification for poetry—imagination—and is therefore a little poem. You might write it like this:
>
> The butterfly
> Is a fairy's golden airplane
> Sailing over the purple flowers.

Much of the verse that we get from children stops at the second stage. I think of it as the pupa stage. If we ask the right questions, we can get the butterfly out of the chrysalis; we need not break the shell and pick it out ourselves. We should ask, "What is it like? What does it look like, or sound like, or feel like? What does it make you think of?"

An older child can be taught that poetry which has feeling is more significant than poetry which stops with presenting an image. How can we get feeling into the poem we have just created? We might ask the child, "How do you feel when you see the butterfly?" Or, "How does the fairy feel?" Or, "How does the butterfly feel being a fairy's airplane?" We should suggest that, in order to keep a unified point of view, he should choose only one of the questions to answer. And we might get something like this:

A fairy is having fun
Sailing his golden butterfly airplane
Over the purple flowers.

Now we have a real poem with both imagination and feeling. The idea is in shape, the image is completed, and the meaning is thought out. Next we may, if we like, turn our attention to rhyme and meter. The poem does not need further patterning; indeed, it has more originality and freshness without it. But if the poet wants rhymes, all he has to do is to rearrange the idea he already has. Any other procedure will usually get rhyme without idea, producing clever verse or jingle, but not poetry. In order to put this poem into rhyme, keeping the imagery, we must do a little juggling and perhaps add another bit to the picture to make the lines come out right:

Over the purple flowers,
In the summer sun,
Sailing his golden butterfly 'plane,
A fairy is having fun.

The following lesson plans have been used successfully with junior-high-school groups:

I. BUILDING AN IMAGE

What is imagination?

Imagination is the picture-forming power of the mind. It is an important quality of poetry. It is the quality that helps you to see the rainbow in a muddy pool, pictures in clouds, or wings on a caterpillar. It helps you to see the beauty and importance of common things. It helps you to share your experiences with other people.

Imagination needs exercise

Imagination needs exercise, just as muscles need exercise. The more often you make a conscious attempt to look at life imaginatively, the more easily you can do so. If you observe carefully all the little things that make up your days and let your imagination play about them, you look at life in the poet's way. Everything that happens becomes intensely interesting.

Images are important

The images that you make to express your observations and ideas give pleasure to the reader as well as to the maker. You share your experiences in beauty and achieve the satisfaction of expressing your own thoughts and feelings in a worthwhile way. You put images into your poems in order to make them more interesting and more beautiful and to help the reader to see things exactly as you have seen them.

What is an image?

An image is a mental picture of an idea. It is a picture formed by the mind, and it is the result of imagination at work. When you see and express likenesses in things that are different, you are making images. These are images:

The sea roars like a lion.
The moon is a silver dollar.
The sailboat was like a white-winged bird.
The stars are sparks from heaven's fire.
The clouds are castles in the sky.

Find the images in the following poems:

RAIN HORSES

Over the mountains
And over the plains,
Small horses clatter their hoofs
When it rains.
–*Jimmie Burnett, age 8*

NIGHT COVERLET

How royal we mortals,
To sleep beneath blue velvet
Embroidered with sparkling jewels.
–*Martha Stagis, age 13*

STORMY WAVES

Stormy waves of wisdom
Crash against the shores of thought
And sweep in knowledge.
–Doris Robinson, age 14

Building the image

After you have chosen your subject, ask yourself the following questions and try to find answers for them. Try to express your answers in interesting words that have color and picture quality.

1. What is it like?
2. How are the two things similar?
3. Of what does it remind me?
4. How do I feel about it? That is, what sort of feeling do I have when I think about it?

Example

Subject: poplar trees at night, in autumn
What are they like? Spider webs across the moon.
How are they similar? The boughs of the leafless trees interlace like the threads of a web.
Of what do they remind me? They set traps to catch the moon.
How do I feel about it? I want to break the web and let the moon escape.

You may make a poem of this by arranging the words in rhythmic and beautiful patterns, as follows:

TREES AT NIGHT

The trees weave magic webs across the moon
With interlacing boughs,
Like giant spiders setting traps
To catch a tasty morsel.
Moon, shall I break the threads
And let you go?

Exercise

Try to write a few lines, containing an image, about something within your own experience. You need not use rhyme. Let your expression be free, and try to find the exact words which will express what you wish to say. The following suggestions may help you to get started, if you cannot think of a subject of your own:

Wind on the water	Boat on the bay	Wind bells
Silver moonlight	Lights on the water	Snowflakes
Shadow of fear	Desert shadow	Helicopter
Hibiscus blooms	Leaf patterns	Jet airplane
City serenade	Storm at sea	April rain

II. BEAUTY IN POETRY

Imagination is most effective in producing artistic expression in poetry when it weaves its magic web with beauty.

When you see a beautiful thing, or hear a beautiful sound, or think of a beautiful idea, you want to share it with others. You may let your imagination play about it until you succeed in turning the experience in beauty into the most artistic form of expression—a poem.

The writing of poetry is an interesting, enjoyable, and valuable experience because it helps to make you conscious of beauty. It helps you to see the beauty in common things and to express the beauty in a way that gives you personal satisfaction. It is a searchlight that shows you beauty in unexpected places.

What is beauty? A thing is beautiful if it is bright and gay and makes you feel happy or pleased when you look at it. Anything that makes you want to draw or paint a picture of it has beauty. Even a cartoon has beauty of line. All the lines fit into each other to make a pattern that pleases your eye. Anything you hear that makes a pleasing sound has beauty. There is beauty in a bird's song, in happy laughter, in the roar of the ocean, in the rhythmic beat of a machine. There is beauty in motion—in the flight of a bird, the wind in the trees, the rise and fall of ocean waves, a cat arching its back. There is beauty in the movements of machinery. Beauty is all about you.

One way you can keep in tune with beauty is to search your surroundings and to examine your experiences for beautiful things. Try to find one beautiful thing each day and to express its beauty in words.

Exercises

1. Think of the most beautiful thing you have ever seen. Try to express its beauty with imagery and picture words that will help others to see exactly how it looked to you. Sell it to them.
2. What is the most beautiful sound you can think of? Use your imagination to produce an image that will express the beauty of that sound.
3. Complete the following images:
   Poppies are like . . .
   The fountain looked like . . .
   The high waves tossed the ship about like . . .
   The midnight sky is like . . .
   The new moon is . . .
   He was as frisky as . . .
   The flames roared through the forest like . . .
   A palm tree against the sky is like . . .
   The humming bird is . . .
   The north wind tossed the trees like . . .
4. Choose one of the following subjects for a poem, and build an image about it.

Bird songs at dawn	Drum beats	Railroad tracks
Winding road	Song of the machine	Apple trees
Mockingbird	High bridge	High dive

These lessons stress the expression of imagination in images and the use of images in poetry. But just any image is not sufficient evidence of the poetic spirit at work. The image must be fresh. It must be the poet's own and not one borrowed from other writings, not a worn-out image that has become tiresome from repetition, that has lost much of its original meaning. When children understand that originality is desired, that their own images are acceptable, they will produce such distinctive expressions as these:

LEAVES

The leaves fall
Like big pennies,
And the sidewalk catches them.
—*Paul Walker, age 6*

THE FOG

The fog looks like smoke
And the bare trees
Like deer horns
Fighting the fog.
–Dale Grimm, age 7

RAINDROPS

Outside the window
The dropping dots of rain
Go pitter patter
Upon the tips of trees.
They hit the houses,
And glancing off,
Spatter like silver glass.
–Dale Griffin, age 7

THE WIND

The wind is like water.
It comes all over me
Like a flood.
–Albert Salcido, age 7

ORANGE

The sun looks like an orange to me.
It hangs up in a blue sky tree.
Cloud branches wave "Good night" to me
And drop the orange in the sea.
–Darleen Greenberg, age 8

CLOUDS ARE CLOWNS

Clouds are clowns
Away up in the sky,
Tumbling all around.
I go up in an airplane
To a circus
Painted blue and silver.
–Sharli Lyon, age 8

RAINDROPS

The raindrops look
Like broken pieces of stars
That have fallen
From the sky.
–Lucia Alice Cheyney, age 9

CLOUDS

The wings of the morning
Are feathery clouds
That sail across the sky
Towing the sun.
–Agnes Gordon, age 9

POWDERED SUGAR

Snow is like powdered sugar
Sprinkled over the mountains.
When the sun comes,
The little streams come trickling down
Like candy syrup.
–Helen Loeb, age 11

SKY'S DRESSES

Sky's mother is a tired old person,
Because Sky plays so much
She tears her frock.
Her mother sits all day long
Sewing white patches on her blue dress.
–Mary Lidyoff, age 11

SNAKE

The wind
Is like a great snake
Hissing in the clouds.
Nobody can stop it.
–Lydia Gonzales, age 12

RAIN CLOUD

Clouds like gray warships
Are stealing silently by
Into the dark night.
—Sam Wilder, age 12

MOON

The moon is a valuable pearl.
It sits upon a velvety sky
With diamond stars all around it,
Placed by God's hand
In His own jewel shop.
—Betty Jean Reiman, age 12

PALM TREES

I love to see the palm trees
Reaching up so high.
They look like great big dusters
Dusting off the sky.
—Pat Christensen, age 13

STARS

Sparks from the candles
On the high altar of night
Glow in the dark sky.
—Leslie H. Walter, age 14

SNOWFLAKES

The snowflakes are falling
On a very cool day;
They are messages from the upper world,
From people far away.
—Margaret Salcido, age 14

WINGS

I know now
How a caterpillar feels
When it gets wings
And soars
Above a blue pool mirror,
A gaudy butterfly.
For I have seen the ocean
From a black and silver airplane.
–Jack Hawkins, age 15

Each of the poems is distinctive for its imagery. When we show children how to use their imagination, we open for them the gate to a whole new field of beauty, a field with unlimited possibilities. Every experience thereafter becomes a creative experience, with its urge to give expression to the thoughts and the feelings it arouses and its reward in personal satisfaction.

3 ❧ Adventures in Beauty

A THING OF BEAUTY

When I have found and loved a thing of beauty
And felt it stir me like a tossing wind,
I live a moment of eternity,
Marked by the silent music in my soul.
–Betsy Caroll, age 16

WE HAVE FOUND IMAGINATION TO be the first essential of poetry and the most important factor in poetry by children. It is most effective in producing artistic expression in poetry when it feeds upon beauty. The desire to share with others the beauty that we have discovered sets imagination to work devising a way to present it so that others will see it, also.

The writing of poetry not only helps us to share the beauty we have found but also makes us conscious of beauties that we might otherwise have missed. It sensitizes our perceptions so that no least manifestation of the beautiful escapes our notice. It helps to make the world interesting and satisfying.

Beauty reveals itself in many forms and in unexpected places. To find beauty we need not go adventuring to some far-off romantic isle in the South Seas. We have only to look about us with a little more conscious attention to detail.

Many people are accustomed to think of beauty as belonging only to that with eye appeal. They have not trained their other senses to apprehend it. The poet has broadened his conception of what is beautiful to include all manifestations that are characteristic of and appropriate to the natural or the human world. The modern poet creates symphonies from the stuff of modern life; he finds the rhythms of a speedy machine age as beautifully significant as the older poet found the slower tempo of his time.

One of the first things children must be taught to do, in their search for beauty, is to examine the details of their environment. Is there in the classroom a bit of color that delights the eye? Is there a plant with little blooms that arouse a feeling of pleased wonder at their tiny perfection? Is there a sketch or a picture with lovely lines and colors? Is there a bird that thrills young ears with its song? Is there a vase or a flower bowl with good lines? From the windows can the children see the blue sky, the mountains, a tree? Can they see butterflies drifting past or hear birds chirping? Can they see a tall building, or smoke rising from chimneys in interesting patterns? Can they hear a train, a bus, a big truck, or a variety of other city noises?

The teacher who through personal experience has arrived at an understanding and appreciation of beauty is best able to lead children in the exploration of the physical environment. The early discoveries of beauty will come through sensory appeals, and the first of these is color, appealing to the visual sense. If a child is asked to point out something beautiful, the chances are that he will point out something with color. The first step toward recognizing beauty will be the realization of the possibilities of color and color combinations. Closely allied to color is the contrast between light and shadow. The more advanced student will find beauty in shade and tint, in line and form.

Beauty in sound is less likely to be discovered by the child without assistance. He will need listening exercises. We might begin with music, with the songs he already knows, and lead into an appreciation of other sounds. We might teach him to listen to sounds in nature—bird songs, insect sounds, the whir of wings, the wind in the leaves, the rain on the roof, the roll of thunder, the spatter of running water, the crackle of fire. Then we should teach him to listen to more complex sounds—city noises, machinery at work, singing telephone wires—and to distinguish between pleasing sounds and harsh, discordant sounds. We should teach him to distinguish between loud sounds and low sounds, high-pitched and low-pitched tones, long sounds and short sounds. The attempt to express these sounds in words, or to express in imagery the effects of the sounds upon the listener, will increase the child's awareness of the beauty of sound.

Of the other three senses—smell, taste, and touch—the last is most likely to appeal to the child as a source of beauty. Little children form their impression of objects by handling them. They are very sensitive to the "feel of things" and are able to distinguish many degrees of softness, smoothness, roughness, and sharpness. They can easily be led to find beauty in textures.

Another source of beauty in the physical environment is motion, manifested in various actions and rhythms. Young children delight in rhythms and enjoy finding the rhythms in various activities of their lives. The rhythm in the flight of a bird, in the running of a dog, in the swaying of a tree in the wind invites imitation and verbal expression.

Finally, we should explore school activities. We may capitalize upon the children's interest in a new picture in the hall, exhibits in the front showcase, auditorium programs and settings, recorded music, or a flower arrangement; and we may watch their appreciation grow as we give them a chance to discover beauty in these experiences.

DEVELOPING STANDARDS

In order to use effectively for poetry the various factors of the physical environment, we must set up certain standards of beauty so that our approach will not be haphazard and our children will not become confused. How are we going to measure beauty? How are we to know what is beautiful and what is not? Are there any absolute values?

To those of us who have had little training in the principles of art, and to children, the attempt to determine what is beautiful is often bewildering. And yet, we all know what we like in color, in shape, in sound, and in movement. Very often the lack of beauty in our surroundings comes from a setting up of false standards, according to what we think we ought to like or according to what we think other people like. We go wrong because we distrust our own instincts or because we want to make an artificial display.

Three little rules should guide us in our selection of the beautiful: (1) comparison with nature, (2) appropriateness, and (3) pleasing effect. In setting up standards of beauty, let us first of all be guided by nature. Even very small children can learn the principle that colors, shapes, and combinations of form and color that occur in nature are pleasing to the esthetic sense. They can study line and form and color at first hand and learn to sharpen their observation for comparison and contrast. They can listen to the sounds of birds and of insects; of twigs and leaves crackling under the feet; of wind whispering or moaning or shrieking through the trees; of rain on the roof, on the leaves, or on the sidewalk. They can learn to distinguish the odors of newly cut grass, of common flowers, of herbs, or of soil after a rain. And they can learn something of texture by feeling the bark of a tree, the leaves of trees and plants, grass, or the satiny petals of a poppy. Every one of these discoveries is a separate adventure in beauty, an adventure that, by teaching the child to see beauty and to understand it, will not only increase his awareness but also deepen his appreciation and open to him another road to personal satisfaction.

The principle of appropriateness applies in all the artificial factors of our environment. Furniture that is too big and clumsy for a small room will not be beautiful in that setting. Heavy, thick coloring on a vase of delicate form is not appropriate. Huge frames on tiny pictures are not appropriate. Thickly bunched flowers in a spindly vase are not appropriate. All the parts of an art arrangement must seem to belong together. Things which have beauty when seen individually may neutralize each other and produce an ugly design, just as colors neutralize each other. We should let children experiment with colored paper and picture mountings until they can see for themselves how backgrounds of color may bring out or may deaden the highlights in a picture. We should show them the relationship between delicate flowers and delicate containers, heavy flowers and pottery bowls. We should show them that sounds and rhythms appropriate to one occasion are not appropriate to another.

A part of the pleasing effect we call beauty is derived from appropriateness, but the remainder comes from balance and proportion. These three in combination produce the harmony we call beauty. In the study of balance and proportion as factors in producing beauty, once again we take nature for our guide. The little child can see proportion in natural objects. The older child can be led to discover balance not only in the shapes and other physical features of objects in nature, but also in the more abstract ideas and ideals connected with natural laws.

Just as children need to be taught before they can read, so they need to be guided into an appreciation of the beautiful. The purpose of our study, therefore, is to show them the trail. We should not arbitrarily list certain beautiful things they are to appreciate because we have decided that these things are beautiful; rather, we should show them how to discover beauty for themselves and to make that beauty a part of their consciousness. Individual growth in awareness and appreciation is our goal.

ADVENTURE IN GREEN

"What is green?"

I waited expectantly. My sixth-graders gave me a pitying look.

"Why, it's just green," somebody ventured. "A color. Everybody knows what green is. Look, it's like my crayon."

"But my crayon is a different green," I pointed out.

"Sure, light green," one of the boys agreed. "There's light green, dark green, and just green, and that's all," he added, positively.

"I'm not sure that's all," I said, turning my eyes toward the windows that opened upon a street beautiful with many varieties of trees and shrubs and plants.

The class quickly took the hint, and that was the beginning of our adventure in exploring Nature's prodigality with her favorite color. We tried first of all to see how many shades of green we could find, collecting small leafy twigs of about the same size. By the time we had exhausted the possibilities of the plant world, we had a row of jars the length of our room, each containing one or more samples of a different shade of green. And what fun we had trying to name those shades. Our stamp collectors contributed some labels, and some were obtained from paint-store folders. A girl whose sister was an artist brought us the names for several shades. And for some we had to make up names.

Of course, the next thing that happened was the discovery that none of the artificial shades exactly matched the natural shades, and there was a great deal of activity with crayons and paint boxes, each child convinced that he could find the right combination. Many were the attempts to paint those twigs exactly as they were in nature.

"Now I see what makes an artist work and work and work all the time trying to get just the right shade," said one, finally. "It's because he never can. I wonder why."

"I know that," our bookworm contributed. "I read it in a book. It's because of something called pigment in our paint. It has to be there to make the color stick, but it isn't pure. The green in the leaves is chlorophyll, made by the sunlight. And the colors in the sky are just light divided up. That's why we can't copy them. We can't ever get them just right."

For a moment everybody was sunk in gloom. Then a little girl brightened. "Well, my goodness!" she exclaimed. "Wouldn't it be awful if we could? It's trying that's fun, because every time you might come a little closer, and then you want to try to beat that."

"Just like racing," a boy commented. "Runners are always trying to beat the record."

"Let's try some word pictures," I suggested, when the interest in painting began to wane. "Here is a sentence from the story Alice wrote last week. 'After the rain everything in the park looked very green.' Do you think it can be improved?"

"Oh, yes!" Alice exclaimed eagerly. "The cedars were blue-green, and the camphor trees were bright green, and the hedge was yellow-green."

"That's just a list of colors," someone pointed out.

"Think of the shapes of your trees," I suggested, "and the way they were placed in relation to one another."

After considerable experiment the class produced this sentence: "The camphor trees, like bright green igloos, squatted in a huddle in front of the yellow-green hedge, and blue-green cedars, like tall church steeples, towered over them." Having discovered that many things we wanted to talk about could be compared or contrasted with our natural greens, we abandoned paints, for the time being, to pursue the new interest in making word pictures.

"If you say, 'He is as green as a camphor tree,' I guess everybody will know what you mean," one of the boys chuckled.

Next, we looked through our books of poetry to see what the poets had done with this green world. The children read their selections aloud and discussed them. They were especially delighted with the imagery in John Gould Fletcher's "Green Symphony," which I read to them. Finally, they made a few images of their own, and some of them wove their images into original poems.

"I think you started something," a little girl informed me, "when you asked us what is green. It will never be just green to me again."

"Every time I pass a tree, I look to see what shade of green it is," another agreed.

Without a doubt, our little adventure had sharpened the observation, stirred the imagination, increased the awareness, and deepened the appreciation of the group. It stimulated interest in other colors as they appear in flowers, in the sunset, and on distant mountains. Children who made trips to the beach were delighted with the many changing colors of the sea. Colors in nature acquired a special significance for them.

From a beginning such as this, one might develop a study of color combinations and the use of the resulting knowledge in flower arrangements, in dress design, in room decoration, in art work, and in word pictures and poems. Every attempt to express beauty is valuable, for it marks growth in observation and appreciation, and by increasing awareness contributes to the development of the child's personality.

ADVENTURE WITH SHADOWS

We had darkened the room for lantern slides, and the light was still on the screen, after the last slide had been shown.

"Look," Juan exclaimed. "I can make my fingers like a rabbit!"

"And I can make my fingers like a dog to chase your rabbit," Miguel laughed.

Of course, everybody wanted to make shadows on the screen, all at the same time. So we took turns. We rolled up the screen, pinned up some paper, and drew around some of the shadows. We had a good time with profiles. Afterwards, we looked about the room for other shadows. With the sun streaming in our south windows, they were not hard to find.

"Everything has a shadow," Alice marveled. "Look at the shadow of these flowers on the table."

"See if you can find any shadows in the flowers themselves," I suggested.

"Oh, yes," she exclaimed. "Look, on the side where the sun does not touch, it is darker."

"When we paint pictures of things, we ought to put in their shadows, too," one of the boys suggested.

The attempt to draw and paint shadows taught us a number of things about them. We discovered that their outlines were often fuzzy and were constantly changing and that sometimes the shadow did not look at all like the original. We went out into the schoolyard to observe our own shadows at different times of the day. We looked at shadows of trees and buildings, of telephone poles, and of parked cars. We discovered that even clouds make shadows. Our next step was to try to look at shadows imaginatively, to tell of what they reminded us, in order to make word pictures and poems.

"Let's make a poem about shadows, all of us together," Mike suggested.

"The shadows are like fingers," said Johnny, promptly.

"That's a good picture," Mary Jane agreed. "Let's say, 'The shadows in the wind,' because fingers move, and the wind makes the trees move."

"The shadows of the trees," Margaret contributed.

"In the wind," Mary Jane insisted.

"Are like fingers," Johnny put in.

"Reach out their fingers," Miguel corrected, "is better."

"Make it 'long fingers,' " Johnny added, as I erased and rewrote to keep up with them.

"They ought to be reaching for something," Alice said thoughtfully.

"They could reach for your feet," Juan pointed out.

"To catch my feet," Evelyn said.

Here is the completed poem:

The shadows of the trees
In the wind
Reach out long fingers
To catch my feet.

Last of all, we had to find a title, finally settling upon "Fingers of Shadow." The following poem was made by the group in much the same way:

PROMISE OF RAIN

The shadow of a cloud
Drifted over my garden
Like a promise
To the thirsty flowers.

By this time pencils were flying over paper as each child hurried to write out some thought of his own. Nor were all the poems about shadows. For the creative mood, once aroused, is likely to go off at a tangent in any direction as one thought or image suggests another. Seeing pictures in shadows led us, naturally, to seeing pictures in clouds, for the sky was plentifully sprinkled with them that day. And soon we had a number of interesting new poems for our class book.

ADVENTURE WITH MACHINES

What about beauty and the machine age? Can we find beauty in a machine? Any boy who has stood in fascination before turning wheels, who has been drawn irresistibly by the glitter and the rhythm of some mechanical device in operation, will answer yes to that question.

As we planned our trip to the tire factory, we decided to see everything we could in order to satisfy our curiosity about that factory, and we were also going to keep our eyes open to see if we could find any sort of beauty that we had not previously noticed. The search began on the bus, when Miguel said, "Listen how it roars, the traffic, just like the waves of the sea."

Everybody listened and nodded agreement. There was an unmistakable rhythm in the roar of sound that continuously rose and receded.

"All the noises have a different tone," said Paul, the musical one. "They are like many instruments all together. You could make a piece for the orchestra to sound like the traffic. On my trombone I could play the streetcar starting."

"A symphony!" Alice exclaimed. "The traffic is a symphony, a modern, jazzy symphony. Oh, that sounds like a poem."

Two or three notebooks and pencils appeared.

"The city moves on wheels," Johnny muttered, writing absorbedly. "I'm going to have a poem about wheels—all kinds of wheels that make everything go."

"What do you call that shiny stuff on the cars?" Mary Jane wanted to know. "I think that's beautiful, the way it flashes in the sunlight."

"Chromium," several boys chorused. "You couldn't make a rhyme with that."

"I don't need a rhyme," Mary Jane retorted. "This traffic noise doesn't sound like a rhyme to me. It's too jittery. I'm going to make my poem jittery to match."

By the time we arrived at the factory, we had found beauty in the crisscross of shiny streetcar rails, in flashing and winking signs, in tall buildings with their many windows like hundreds of eyes, in the colorful pageant of milling crowds. The factory itself offered a new field for speculation.

"How can you find anything beautiful in dirty old machinery?" several girls complained.

"You just stand there and watch it doing work all by itself," said Joe, the quiet one. "It isn't how it looks that counts. See, it never misses."

In the tire factory there were so many interesting processes to be observed that we were soon very busy listening to our guide and trying not to miss anything. It was a time for observation rather than for creation, and notebooks were gradually tucked away.

However, the days following the trip were productive not only of stories, reports, exhibits, and drawings, but also of poems that showed imagination at work. As usual with the creative mood, the tire factory was only a point of departure, for one image suggested another until we had poems about many different phases of industrial activity.

"Streetcars are beautiful, and cars are beautiful, and trains are beautiful," Johnny maintained. "Everything is beautiful that goes on wheels."

"It is not how it looks that is beautiful," Alice said thoughtfully. "I see now that it is the way it works."

"And what it does for the world—that, too, is important," Miguel insisted. "Think how steel has changed the world. You could make a poem about steel."

"A great poet did," said our bookworm. "Wait, I'll find it in the book and show you. His name is Carl Sandburg. He wrote about smoke and steel and factories and cities and all kinds of things like that."

Our adventure with machines opened the eyes of the children to a new type of beauty and made them more aware of and more appreciative of the industrial world than they had been before. Having seen the beauty, the fascination, the poetry in labor, they should find no job in their grown-up future so lacking in interest as to produce the boredom that leads to discontent or to failure.

FINGER EXERCISES

The purpose of our study, which is individual growth in awareness and appreciation, can best be achieved by children who express in creative activity what beauty means to them. One advantage of poetry as a creative activity is that it uses words rather than expensive materials. Furthermore, a child's attempt to verbalize his experiences expands his emotional and intellectual horizons. It develops his ability to communicate as well as his ability to understand the communications of others. It opens a door to the appreciation of a very important part of his cultural heritage.

In order to express adequately and satisfactorily his responses to experience, the writer of poetry must continually practice with words as the musician practices exercises to develop skill in his fingers.

Before attempting to teach children to put beauty into their own verse, we should let them discover it in poetry as well as in art and nature. To primary children we should read aloud a great deal of poetry—not just humorous jingle, but poetry that has in it the imaginative qualities we hope to develop in their own expressions. We should help them to enjoy the pictures as well as the rhythms and to discover the words that help to create the pictures.

Above the primary level we should put into the hands of the children copies of some of the poems we use for poetry-appreciation lessons, so that they may select beautiful lines, strong lines, and favorite lines, as well as specific images and interesting words. We can increase their discernment by suggesting that they look for a beautiful picture, for an interesting phrase, for specific sensory appeals, for enjoyable rhythms, and for lines worth remembering. This attention to detail will help to point out and focus attention upon the beauties of the poem and upon its significant ideas. The following "finger exercises" may be helpful in starting a creative writing project with emphasis on beauty:

EXERCISES

1. Complete the following images:
   As red as . . .
   As blue as . . .
   As yellow as . . .
   As white as . . .
   As green as . . .
2. Try naming imaginatively the colors in rocks.
3. Try naming imaginatively the shapes of seashells.
4. Listen to the sounds of nature in the woods, in the park, or in your own yard at night. How many can you find? How many can you name? What do they make you think of?
5. Listen to the song of a bird, and try to describe it imaginatively.
6. Watch the way a pigeon walks and the tracks it makes. Make an image to describe it.
7. Of what does the odor of sweet peas (or any other available flower) remind you? Make an image.
8. Look for textures. How many different textures can you discover in the classroom? Try to describe them in images.
9. Try to describe in images the taste of an onion, pepper, candy, ice cream, sour pickles.
10. Make three images of motion.
11. Select three different color schemes that appear in nature, and try to describe them in verse.
12. Lay your hand on a piece of paper, and draw around it. Then describe it imaginatively.
13. Draw the picture suggested by a poem that has been read aloud to you.
14. Choose a picture, and write a poem about it.

In our attempt to focus on beauty, we must remember that the beauty we are seeking is best expressed or implied in the imagery of a poem. The image should be so graphic that an artist reading the poem would be able to paint the picture. He should be able to discover the objects to put into his picture and the colors to use. It is not enough just to name ordinary colors; the poet must give his colors individuality by analogy and contrast.

We should not, however, urge and prod children into putting beauty into their poetry, lest they fall into the error of listing objects or of sacrificing sense to beauty. Rather, we should lead them to see that beauty in itself is not the end and aim of writing poetry, but only the means to the end, which is *self-expression*. We should show them that the mere mention of beauty or of some of its attributes will not make a complete poem, any more than the collection of paint tubes will make the picture. As the brush of the artist must mix and apply the colors, so the mind of the poet must seek and express the *significance* of the beauty he sees.

The poet must be concrete. It is not enough to say, "How beautiful the stars are." That conveys no picture to the mind of the reader. How much better it is to make pictures like these:

DESERT MAGIC

When you are on a desert,
The stars shining brightly
Look like little silver spiders
Hanging on long, thin threads,
Reaching down to you.
–Mary Lidyoff, age 12

GOD'S HOME

In the daytime
The clouds look like silver carpets
On which the Lord sits.
In the night, the blackness
Looks like a great blanket,
And the stars are tiny crystals
Sewed into it.
The moon is God's pillow.
–Ralph and Trent Cheyney, age 10

STARS

Stars are fireflies,
Stars are lights
From the homes
Of clouds at night.
Stars are chips
Of moon, I bet;
Stars are dreams
That I forget.
—Donna Jean Smith, age 12

In the following poem the delicate beauty of apple blossoms is very deftly suggested by the use of concrete detail. The reader feels that the young poet has caught and held in her poem the fragrance and the fleeting loveliness of apple blossoms and drifting petals.

THE FAIRIES AND THE APPLE BLOSSOMS

In May I love my apple tree;
Its blossoms pink and white
Make party frocks for fairy folk
Who dance in pale moonlight.

The petals do not always fit,
And that is why I found
So many bits and scraps today
All scattered on the ground.
—Shirley Banks, age 13

The girl who wrote "Hula Dancer" made her picture come to life for us by her use of vivid phrasing and concrete imagery. She has proved to us that beauty may be found in a stormy day as well as in the calm peace of a bright, sunny day.

HULA DANCER

The sky looks gloomy.
The clouds look like icebergs
Floating in the air up above us.
The wind makes the trees sway
Back and forth,
Like the skirt of a hula dancer.
The sun shines through the clouds
Like a spotlight
On the little dancer.
–Ofelia Montana, age 13

The author of "Cathedral Candle" found beauty in a single candle, and has given that beauty a deep significance by placing her candle in a church. Tying up her imagery with two emotional concepts, she presents a poem that not only points out, but also interprets beauty in a satisfying way.

CATHEDRAL CANDLE

A cathedral candle
Glimmers and gleams
Like beautiful dreams.
A cathedral candle
Is like a prayer.
When the world is asleep,
It is still gleaming there.
–Esther Glasgow, age 13

A small thing may attract the interest of a mind attuned to beauty. The beauty of a seagull against the sky inspired the following poem:

SAILBOATS IN THE SKY

Whirling, wheeling whiteness,
Fairy, feathery lightness
Sailing swiftly by,
Sailboats in the sky.
Proud and silent majesty
Calling, racing happily—
Seagulls flying by,
Sailboats in the sky.
–Shirley Scholz, age 13

In the following poem we find an unusual combination of details. The beauty of sound is expressed in visual images.

MUSIC

Dutch music
Makes me think of clattering shoes,
Girls churning cheese,
Playing among colorful tulips.

Arabian music
Makes me think of gorgeous ladies
With silks and satins,
Snow-white laces,
Men on camels' backs,
Softness of the night.

African music
Makes me think of freedom,
The wild beasts,
The great children of God.

American music
Makes me think of snowy mountain caps,
Red hot deserts,
And blue oceans.

The softness of music
Makes me think of sweet children
In the flowers.
–Gloria Jarboe, age 10

4 Emotional Values in Poetry

TOO YOUNG?

I am too young, they say, to know this pain.
(Their fingers tear the butterfly apart.)
Perhaps I am. And yet, I feel that rain
Clatters like drops of doom upon my heart.
—*Angela Mendoza, age 15*

THE BASIS OF POETRY IS EMOTIONAL rather than intellectual. The communal origins of our poetry indicate that our tribal ancestors expressed themselves in rhythms, not as an intellectual exercise but as a method of emotional release. The purpose of their tribal songs and rhythms was to express their reactions to experience, or to direct and inspire activities in which the tribe was interested. Primitive peoples realized early the value of the war song and dance in stirring up sufficient hatred to induce their warriors to kill. They fostered tribal pride and courage and a sense of tribal unity by celebrating in song and verse the great deeds of their tribal heroes. The earliest rhythms were developed out of a need to express triumph over an enemy, to stir up hatred of an enemy, to express pride in the achievements of heroes, and to propitiate unknown and much-feared elemental forces.

Our incentives have changed very little. Our poems still express all sorts of triumphs over others, over ourselves, over elemental forces, over life's vicissitudes. They still stir people to hatred of injustice, of cruelty, of wartime enemies. They still sing of heroes and their accomplishments.

All true poetry is motivated by emotion. A poem does not come into being until an inner emotional compulsion moves a poet to put his thoughts and feelings into words. The poet's mission is threefold: (1) to express an emotion adequately and artistically for his own personal satisfaction, (2) to share his emotional experiences with others, (3) to stir an emotional response in the reader.

When we read poetry, we seek to share the poet's emotional experience or to find in such experiences a reflection of our own. The poem is emotionally satisfying that stirs a feeling of personal kinship or agreement with the author, allows the reader to share an emotional experience, or awakens a desire for self-expression.

Emotional appeal is very closely related to imagination and rhythm. The deeper the poet's feeling about his subject, the more figurative his language becomes and the more rhythmical is his expression. But when the author makes the intellectual rather than the emotional approach, his poem may be characterized by insincerity, uncertainty of rhythm, and prosy didacticism, and these weaknesses may prevent its making an impact on the reader.

The poet achieves his purpose by the use of words to express and to arouse feeling, and by images and the ideas associated with them. He selects words not only for their exactness of meaning, but also for their connotations. Words have value for poetry not only because of what they say but also because of their power to arouse emotional response.

DEVELOPING EMOTIONAL UNDERSTANDING

In order to develop in children a true appreciation of poetry, we must make sure that they understand it with their emotions as well as with their minds. Much of the dislike that children acquire for poetry is due to their complete lack of emotional understanding. They have no sense of personal sympathy with the poet's problem nor comprehension of his motives, and they are not stirred by his music. Perhaps their bewilderment is really our fault. We do not expect children to understand music or art by instinct; but we seem to expect them to arrive unaided at a proper appreciation of poetry, which is fully as difficult as either music or art. We offer them no emotional guideposts, and often we try to put poetry among those things we do for duty's sake rather than among the appreciations. No wonder we turn them against it.

When we read poetry with real understanding, we seek to share the poet's emotional experiences or to find in his experiences a reflection of our own. In order to give children the deep personal satisfaction that comes from such sharing, we must direct their attention to poems with relatively simple emotional concepts suitable to their degree of maturity. We must teach them to recognize the emotional qualities in the poems they hear and read. A sympathetic reading by the teacher will go a long way toward making possible such recognition.

Conscious attention to the emotional content of poetry should begin at the junior-high-school level. At lower-grade levels children may sense a poet's mood, and they may understand with their minds the feeling that prompted a poet to write as he did. They may be able to find poems in which the poet feels like singing, dancing, laughing, shouting, or running. They may recognize feelings of happiness, sorrow, or fear. But they seldom identify themselves emotionally with the mood as an adolescent does. In their own writing we may expect sincerity of feeling, but not depth of feeling. Their immaturity and their difficulties with the mechanics of expression inhibit emotional responsiveness. Any insistence upon emotional content may force them into superficiality or imitative sentimentality.

As children enter the teens, however, they begin to take an interest in relationships with other people and in their own feelings about things. In presenting poetry to them we try to help them discover not only what the poet is saying but also what he is feeling as he writes. We encourage reflection and try to awaken the sympathetic understanding that will evoke the desired response: a feeling of personal kinship or agreement with the author, a sharing of the emotional experience, and a desire for self-expression.

One way to develop emotional understanding in high-school students is to read aloud poems that have simple emotional connotations and to ask the listeners to determine the emotional motivation of each. The following list may be helpful:

Dominant emotion: Joy of Living
- "High Flight" by John Magee, Jr.
- "Pippa Passes" by Robert Browning
- "The Great Lover" by Rupert Brooke
- "The Solitary Reaper" by William Wordsworth
- "Happy Wind" by W. H. Davies
- "I Meant to Do My Work Today" by Richard Le Gallienne

Dominant emotion: Brotherly Love
- "Abou Ben Adhem" by Leigh Hunt
- "Mending Wall" by Robert Frost
- "The People, Yes" by Carl Sandburg

Dominant emotion: Compassion
- "Hurt No Living Thing" by Christina Rossetti
- "The Bells of Heaven" by Ralph Hodgson
- "To a Mouse" by Robert Burns
- "The Last Leaf" by Oliver Wendell Holmes
- "The Death of the Hired Man" by Robert Frost
- "The Cry of the Children" by Elizabeth Barrett Browning

Dominant emotion: Love of Nature
- "I Wandered Lonely as a Cloud" by William Wordsworth
- "Loveliest of Trees" by A. E. Housman
- "To a Skylark" by Percy Bysshe Shelley
- "Ode to the West Wind" by Percy Bysshe Shelley
- "The Cloud" by Percy Bysshe Shelley
- "To One Who Has Been Long in City Pent" by John Keats
- "The Windhover" by Gerard Manley Hopkins

Dominant emotion: Indignation
- "The Man with the Hoe" by Edwin Markham
- 'The Song of the Shirt" by Thomas Hood
- "The Factories" by Margaret Widdemer
- "Old Ironsides" by Oliver Wendell Holmes
- "Does It Matter?" by Siegfried Sassoon
- "On the Late Massacre in Piedmont" by John Milton

Dominant emotion: Response to Beauty
- "Ode on a Grecian Urn" by John Keats
- "The Rhodora" by Ralph Waldo Emerson
- "God's World" by Edna St. Vincent Millay
- "Pied Beauty" by Gerard Manley Hopkins
- "I Died for Beauty" by Emily Dickinson

"Silver" by Walter de la Mare
"Hymn to Intellectual Beauty" by Percy Bysshe Shelley
"Night Clouds" by Amy Lowell
"Nocturne in a Deserted Brickyard" by Carl Sandburg
"Dawn" by William Carlos Williams
"Daisy" by William Carlos Williams
"The Skaters" by John Gould Fletcher
"Symphony in Yellow" by Oscar Wilde
"My Heart Leaps Up" by William Wordsworth
"She Walks in Beauty" by Lord Byron

Dominant emotion: Courage

"Invictus" by William E. Henley
"Prayers of Steel" by Carl Sandburg
"Opportunity" by Edward Rowland Sill
"Do You Fear the Wind?" by Hamlin Garland
"The Old Stoic" by Emily Brontë
"Whatever Odds There Are" by Grantland Rice

Dominant emotion: Love of the Sea

"The Sea Gypsy" by Richard Hovey
"Sea Fever" by John Masefield
"Sonnet on the Sea" by John Keats
"Christmas at Sea" by Robert Louis Stevenson
"Young Sea" by Carl Sandburg
"Sea Charm" by Langston Hughes

Dominant emotion: Romantic Love

"A Birthday" by Christina Rossetti
"The Night Has a Thousand Eyes" by Francis William Bourdillon
"How Do I Love Thee?" by Elizabeth Barrett Browning
"The Ragged Wood" by W. B. Yeats
"Annabel Lee" by Edgar Allan Poe
"A Red, Red Rose" by Robert Burns
"Lochinvar" by Sir Walter Scott
"Love's Philosophy" by Percy Bysshe Shelley
"Spring Night" by Sara Teasdale

Dominant emotion: Religious Faith and Fervor

"The Hound of Heaven" by Francis Thompson
"Holy Sonnets" by John Donne
"A Hymn to God the Father" by John Donne
"Crossing the Bar" by Alfred Lord Tennyson
"I Never Saw a Moor" by Emily Dickinson
"The Spacious Firmament on High" by Joseph Addison
"The Eternal Goodness" by John Greenleaf Whittier

After the students have learned to recognize the dominant emotion in a poem, they may examine the lines to find out specific ways in which the author conveys his feeling to the reader, through rhythm, meter, imagery, allusions, and the use of words with emotional connotations.

OBTAINING THE EMOTIONAL RESPONSE

I am not suggesting that we play upon the emotions of children, deliberately stir them up, or, by a process of hothouse forcing, obtain the expression of a too-mature emotional response. We must remind ourselves once more of our goal: the natural child expressing himself in a natural way. But as the child matures, his emotional life unfolds and becomes more involved and his emotional experiences become more complex; our teaching, therefore, should recognize the tendency toward individual growth and provide something for it to feed upon. We should offer him many experiences in sharing and in creating, so that he will achieve the emotional orientation necessary to the development of a wholesome personality.

It is possible to determine how much and what sort of emotional response may be expected from children at various age levels. The child under twelve years of age will usually not be concerned with social problems or social injustice. He will pay very scant attention to the relations of people to each other or to himself. His approach to the universe, to nature, and to his own experiences will be objective. He will be more likely to write about the appearance of natural phenomena than about their significance. Because he has not yet begun to develop a philosophy of life, his poetry is more likely to be poetry of observation and analogy than poetry of idea or abstraction. Creation in the primary grades is largely the unconscious expression of the child's immediate unreflecting reaction to objects. Emotional experiences play very little part in creative expression at this age level.

But upper-grade children are beginning to notice that experiences affect them in different ways, that certain things give them a happy feeling, others give them a feeling of wonder, and still others make them sad. They can be taught that the greatest poetry shows some of the author's own feelings, and they can be encouraged to ask themselves when they write, "How does it make me feel?" Since their approach to experience, however, is still largely objective, their emotional responses will be objectively expressed. We may expect from these children of ten to twelve years *sincerity* of feeling but not *depth* of feeling.

The sixth-grade child is content to write about the appearances of things, but these do not satisfy the adolescent, who longs to know what the world is all about. He puts into poetry some of his longing, some of his questions, some of his surmises and hopes and aspirations. His poetry is no longer purely objective. His subject matter includes eager speculation about the relations of things to each other, of people to things, of people to people, and of people to the hidden forces of the universe. The distinguishing characteristic of adolescent work in poetry is an awakening awareness to the emotional self. Poetry may act as a safety valve, an emotional outlet, a means of sifting impressions of things and arriving at their true significance and their relativity. What the adolescent needs more than anything else is a sense of relativity and the ability to see himself and his concerns in their proper perspective. He must reflect before he can compose, and reflection, as well as the very act of composition, helps him to set his mental and emotional perceptions in order and gives him the much-needed objective approach to himself. The feeling of satisfaction that comes with the completion of a bit of creative work is a wholesome antidote for his uncertainty about many things. It is this uncertainty, this feeling of incompleteness, that causes the adolescent to begin so many things that he never finishes, to jump from one quick enthusiasm to another as each one leaves him with a baffled feeling. His search for emotional security sometimes becomes rather hectic. And he has no way of knowing that the answer is in himself, or that others have felt the same way.

Much poetry is concerned with emotional struggle and with the triumphant solution of some emotional problem, a point of view that the adolescent is quick to understand and from which he can absorb comfort. If he can put a bit of his own problem into words, can fit it into a pattern of beauty, he arrives at the feeling of peace that comes with any adequate expression of self. Poetry thus helps him to orient himself in his changing, often frightening world, and to find his place in the universal scheme of things; and it helps him to realize that his problems are human problems and not peculiar to himself.

We can expect in senior-high-school students a deepening of perceptions and impressions, with a consequent enrichment of emotional content in their creative work. The younger students may exhibit much of the turmoil and flightiness of the junior-high-school group. But the older students will produce work in which we begin to detect the formation of a philosophy of life, a broadening of emotional perspective, and an awakening of interest in others, with a corresponding slackening of the previous all-absorbing interest in self. Building upon the work of earlier years, we can expect from this group real manifestations of the creative spirit—poetry that is strong, courageous, forward-looking; poetry that promises well for the intellectual future of the race; poetry that reveals the culmination of years of encouragement and effort in an integrated, mentally healthy personality.

Under ideal conditions the emotional response outlined as probable for each age level will be forthcoming. Under usual conditions it will be suppressed rather than expressed, and it may be manifest in inhibitions, exhibitionism, attention-seeking, and other unfortunate types of behavior. Our task as teachers is to encourage by every means available to us constructive self-expression. Creative poetry is suggested not as the cure for all emotional ills, but as one method of relief for emotional colic.

Getting the patient to take the medicine is the initial difficulty. How can we obtain emotional response from our high-school classes? First of all, we should read aloud serious, thoughtful, questioning poetry that has universal appeal, poetry that offers emotional experiences to be shared. We should familiarize the students with the matter and manner of great poetry and show them that human beings down through the ages have found poetry a method of saying what they wish to say about things, of sharing with others ideas that seem worth saving. We should build up in the group a feeling of complete confidence in the teacher as their guide and friend, one who will take them seriously and respect their ideas, their feelings, and their attempts at self-expression. They should feel sure that the teacher is sympathetic and that he will not laugh at them. A child will begin to express his intimate thoughts and feelings when we have convinced him that it is worthwhile to put them into imaginative, artistic form, that his own original ideas are important, and that we respect his efforts.

AVOIDING SENTIMENTALITY

Children are imitative. Very young children, if let alone and allowed to express themselves freely, are not likely to overemotionalize. But as soon as they are able to read for themselves, they are going to be introduced, by way of cheap publications, to moralistic and mawkish verse. Well-meaning but uninformed friends and relatives, as soon as they learn that Johnny has "done a poem" at school, will be full of suggestions for more poems for Johnny to write. Some of them will even undertake to help him write them. The result is likely to be the sort of thing that Johnny, left alone, would never think of writing for himself—sentimental, jingly, and wholly unnatural. Verse writing, instead of a way of expressing his own personality, will become to Johnny a means of appearing clever.

In our teaching we must guard against overemphasizing emotional values and against the tendency to sentimentalize. We must remember that sentimentalism is distinctly an adult reaction, that the child who turns to sentimentalizing is aping the adult and is not being natural or sincere. In order to avoid this pitfall, we shall need to know the difference between poetry and verse.

The test is really very simple: the difference between poetry and verse is imagination; the difference between emotion and sentiment is sincerity. A versifier uses commonplaces cleverly and capitalizes on the platitudes, the trite old ways of thought, and the clichés of language. His verses say nothing new. They are often sentimental, and the sentiment, following an old convention, is false, with no basis in true emotion. Whenever a versifier expresses himself emotionally about an insignificant object or expresses more emotion than the experience warrants, he is sentimentalizing. When he attributes human feelings to inanimate objects, he is sentimentalizing. He is only slightly less obnoxious when he moralizes. True poetry does not have an obvious moral tacked on at the end, after the manner of a fable. The purpose of poetry is to express one's own personality and not to reform others.

A poet, instead of saying the trite and expected about an experience, lets his mind play about it until he discovers hitherto unthought-of analogies, until he sees comparisons that communicate his experience in imaginative, colorful, graphic terms. He uses figurative language because of its vividness and economy. He uses original simile, metaphor, or personification to present a new and different image. He offers either an entirely new thought or an old idea expressed in a new way. His work is a significant contribution to literature, and not just a rehash of what others have said a dozen times over.

These statements, of course, apply only to serious poetry and to verse that pretends to be serious poetry. Light or humorous verse, which naturally does not claim to be poetry, stands in a classification by itself. But to be good, it must also be fresh and original. Nothing falls so flat as worked-over humor.

While the child's poem may make no significant contribution to literature, it may have all the other qualifications of true poetry. The best way to obtain a natural, wholesome, sincere expression from a child is to emphasize the verbalization of his own original ideas and soft-pedal the notion that he must produce a finished poem. His attempt to write a poem that looks or sounds well, whether or not he has any ideas to put into it, is fatal to originality and distorts the whole purpose of the teaching of poetry, which is to develop the creative rather than the imitative tendency.

Furthermore, we must be careful of overpraise and overstimulation. A quiet word of appreciation, when merited, will act as a spur to greater effort. But undeserved or more-than-deserved praise will make the child at first uncomfortable and then vain, and it will distort his perspective. The idea behind creative writing is individual growth, not exhibitionism. Overstimulation causes the child to try to produce poetry faster than ideas come to him, and the result is bound to be inferior. He must be made to understand that his original poetry is not something to be marveled at as the work of a prodigy, but a natural and to-be-expected childhood expression. It is fun to try to write poetry, just as it is fun to try to paint pictures. One does not necessarily expect to become a great poet any more than one who paints a picture in school expects to become a great artist. But painting pictures with words helps one to understand and appreciate the word pictures of other people and to learn what it takes to make a real poem.

We shall not be in danger of developing a superficial attitude toward poetry, or of accepting sentimentalized, moralized, inadequate verse as poetry, if we keep always in mind the fact that we are not trying to make poets of children; we are trying through poetry to help them to express and to develop their personalities. We are trying to build up self-confidence by teaching them to respect their own ideas, to increase observation and stimulate original thinking, to open their eyes to the wonders of the world about them, to deepen their appreciation of the beautiful and the significant, to become interested in the thought processes of others and thus to become interesting persons themselves. We are offering them poetry as a safety valve for the release of emotional tensions that develop when too much is done *for* and not enough is done *by* children.

The following examples show how children express emotion in their poetry and what sort of emotion they are most likely to express. Although the emotional approach is rare in the poetry of younger children, now and then it does occur. The emotion in the first poem is sympathy. Even at seven years of age, a child sometimes can understand the desire for freedom and feel sorry for fettered things.

THE BIRD'S PRISON

The leaf in the tree,
Sticking to a branch,
Was flying back and forth
Like a bird.
I wished the bird could get away
And be happy.
–*Billy Walker, age 7*

Unhappiness to the five-year-old is associated with crying. The strange, unhappy sound of the ocean, therefore, is to him like crying. The emotion is implied rather than expressed, but it is there.

LISTEN!

The ocean cries
Far away in the distance.
It cries and cries.
The wind makes it cry
By blowing.
–*Purjes Russell, age 5*

In comparison with the usual inanities of the Mother's Day poem, with its trite, conventional expressions, the following poem shows both the simplicity of a child's real feeling and sincerity of expression:

MOTHER

Mother, Mother,
You are as sweet as sweet peas
That grow in my garden.
I love you.
–*Toshiko Goto, age 9*

Variety in emotion and the emotional approach to experience take a more prominent place in the poetry of adolescence. Teen-age boys and girls are beginning to understand relationships, to wonder about the meanings of things, and to be aware of social and emotional problems. We can expect to find in their verses the emotions of wonder, awe, sympathy, protest, faith, doubt, and love. Only in rare cases, however, will they attempt to interpret the emotion. Interpretation comes with maturity, after the young poet has solved some of his problems or found the road that leads toward their solution, after he has begun to develop his philosophy of life and thinks that he has some of the answers to the questions that plague humanity. The following examples show the sort of emotional approach that is usually made by teen-age boys and girls. The emotion in the first poem is plainly remorse:

IGNORED

Was I tolerant of pain?
Was I heeding of your word?
No! I blindly stumbled on
As though I had not heard.
–*Constance Johnston, age 13*

In the next poem the poet expresses the age-old desire of man for security. He must find something firm and strong and enduring to bolster his own weak faith. He yearns for the protection of something stronger than himself and looks upon the mountains as symbols of that something. The emotion here is a reaffirmation of faith.

SYMBOLS OF STRENGTH

When the ball of gold is going down,
And the head and heart are weary,
Look toward the mountains for peace and
contentment,
For they are the symbols of strength
and eternity.
–Elroy Duran, age 12

The following poems demonstrate the ability of a poet to identify himself with another and to reproduce the other's emotion. They express the mixed bewilderment, disillusion, relief, and bitterness of the common soldier under fire.

ARMISTICE DAY, 1918

We just call it Armistice Day—
They call it day, hour, minute, second.
Until then, when the time came,
Some called it a joke.
Others called it The Judgment Day.
It was so quiet, like the grave—
Then you could hear the sound of cheers!
You wouldn't see your buddies go down
Under the touch of lead.
This was the time you had waited for—
No more bombs bursting—it was too quiet.
It couldn't be real.
Four years of it. Now it was over!
We knew it was real—Armistice Day, 1918!
–Robert Ward, age 13

HERO'S DUTY

Dot . . . dot . . . dash . . .
   Goes the Morse code,
As I lie in the barren fields
   By the empty road.
Oh! Why can't I answer it?
   Why can't I rise?
One minute I am almost up;
   The next I am down,
With my face in the dirt,
   My hands pounding the ground.
There! I have made it.
   I have answered my call.
My arms are weary, and my legs are, too.
   It doesn't matter now if I fall.
      –Diane Brownstein, age 14

THE DYING SOLDIER

Today I am wounded, and I lie
Dreaming of the days gone by,
Thinking of my life-long story.
Ah, yes, those were the days of glory,
When I was young, and gallant, too.
Today I am worn, and feeling blue,
Lying here, looking at the sky,
Knowing that tomorrow I die.
   –Albert Morales, age 15

Here is another example of that most difficult feat—the identification of self with another and the consequent ability to understand and portray sympathetically the emotional state of another. The emotion is, on the surface, excitement over the events of the game; the underlying emotion is, of course, pride in the hero-son.

A FOOTBALL GAME

Hurrah! He's going to try to score!
Now the game is zero to four.
The crowds are cheering and crying for joy;
He's made a touchdown, this big boy!
Now the game is six to four.
All the crowds are cheering for more,
While slowly the clock is ticking away;
One more minute left to play!
There goes the bell—
Hear that crowd yell!
A lady cries, "We've won, we've won!
He made that touchdown—he, my son!"
–*Janice Rosenfeld, age 14*

In the foregoing verses attention was called to the young poets' apprehension of universal emotional problems. But the problems of adolescence are no less important; they appear very frequently in verse that is honestly and sincerely the expression of the writer's intimate thoughts and feelings. The emotion of loneliness is universal, but it is particularly strong at the adolescent period when the boy or girl is just beginning to realize his or her individuality. Here is a poem expressing that emotion:

NEW SCHOOL

Strange faces all around you,
A lonesome feeling in your heart;
Friends speak and greet each other;
You stand alone, apart.
Tears well up in your eyes—
A stranger smiles at you.
The lonesomeness is gone;
You have a friend, too.
–*Lorraine Moran, age 15*

The following poem expresses the regret that occasionally overtakes the young person who suddenly realizes that he is leaving childhood behind. It is an emotion common to all of us but usually not recognized by one so young.

GROWING-UP BLUES

I've got those growing-up blues.
No more dolls my heart to cheer,
No more jam my face to smear,
No more goblins my soul to fear;
I'm growing up.

I've got those growing-up blues.
No more parties of cookies and tea,
No more fairies in dreams to see,
No more chasing the wandering bee:
I'm growing up.

I've got those growing-up blues.
No more lullabies to sing,
No more rides at the pony ring,
No more Sunday School bells to ring:
I'm growing up.

I've got those growing-up blues.
No more days of childhood fun,
No more meeting Dad when day is done,
No more days to dance and run:
I've grown up.

–Barbara Windette, age 15

The ability to identify self with another is again evident in the following. There is a poignancy in these lines that strikes directly at the heart of the reader. The emotion here is more than sympathy; it is protest at the inhumanity of war. It is a cry for security. It is a child's plea for children, and its unaffected sincerity makes it doubly effective.

A DEAD CHILD'S PRAYER

Dear God,
I am a child of the dead.
I know the horror of war;
Please let there be no more.
I have seen children die,
Heard their agonizing cry;
For I am a child of the dead.
If peace should come,
And all the wrong of war
Should be undone,
I still shall be
A child of the dead.
–George Warga, age 14

The author of "Sanctuary" has found security in nature. Reverence and faith in the goodness of nature and of God are evident in her lines.

SANCTUARY

I spent a day among the hills,
A day among the flowers;
I spent a day in woodland ferns,
A day of happy hours.
I spent a day among the birds,
Among the goldenrod;
I walked beneath the whispering pines;
I spent a day with God.
–Kathryn Jean Ainsworth, age 13

The yearning for freedom is an emotion not limited to adolescence. The conflict between the individual and the social self is an ever-present emotional problem. The protest at social fetters is, however, typical of adolescence, and here we have it graphically expressed:

IF I WERE FREE

The wind knocks at my door,
The rain prances round,
Calling—calling me.
But I am shut within the walls
Of a grim, blackened town.
Oh, if only I were free!
Over the meadows, over the sea,
Heeding not the rain,
While lightning strikes across the sky,
I would go in glee.
But I am between blackened walls,
While my soul yearns.
Oh, if I were only free!
–Constance Johnston, age 13

Even love gets a little attention, and probably gets much more in the poems we never see.

LOVE

How much do I love you?
I cannot say.
Why, why is it,
When I see you coming,
I turn and go the other way?
–Frederico Velasquez, age 15

CAPACITY

My heart is only a few inches square.
It seems there isn't room in there
To hold all the joy and the love I know;
I'm sure there's more room, but it just
doesn't show.
–Rosegene Rasey, age 13

To summarize: our task, as teachers, is not to stimulate emotion or the expression thereof, but merely to recognize it when it appears, to note signs of mental and emotional strain; to encourage the child to think through his problems and to be true to himself.

5 Ideas in Poetry

MAKING A POEM

Idea came knocking
At the door of my mind.
I welcomed him with music,
And together
We made a poem.
—Matsuko Toyama, age 11

POETRY OWES ITS HIGH POSITION IN literature to its ability to present ideas and truths concisely and imaginatively. The poet has an advantage over the prose writer because he can make more significant use of emotional appeal and rhythm to present his idea; but he must have an idea as the reason for his use of emotion, rhythm, and imagination. He must present either a *new* idea or a *new approach* to an old idea. In devising significant imagery for greater impact, the poet contributes not only to the art of poetry, but also to the science of thought. The tempering of ideas in the fire of imagery fanned by emotion leads him into the formulation and the sharing of a philosophy of life. His poetry stirs in the reader the urge to go beyond the poet, to discover the meaning of life for himself, to take his own trail into Infinity.

IDEAS IN THE POETRY OF CHILDREN

The formation of a philosophy of life comes with maturity; it is not to be expected of children. Children can be taught, however, that poetry should present either a new idea or a new approach to an old idea. They can be taught to avoid the commonplace, the remembered, and the imitative; and they can be taught to think about an object or an experience until they find original ways of expressing themselves.

If a child looks at the moon and thinks of some analogy that is different, something that has not been said before, something that explains artistically and imaginatively, in terms of his own personality, what the moon means to him, he is making an intellectual contribution to poetry, and his verse has true poetic value. It does not have such value if he has merely echoed what others have said. In the following poem the intellectual contribution is the unusual imagery:

BABY MOON

The moon
Is like a fat baby.
Every night she comes out
To drink her wind
And smile at us.
–Teno Ruiz, age 13

The intellectual contribution in the next poem lies not in the imagery or the idea expressed but in the implication:

HIS VICTORY

This crippled soldier could walk and run;
He could even shoot a gun.
But now he lies there, still and great:
He won his victory.
His brother is killed, his sister dead,
And he just lies there in his bed.
He says, "Life doesn't mean a thing to me,
But I won my victory."
–Marie Harris, age 12

All of the tragedy, the futility of war, and the hollowness of victory, as well as the waste of human life and the irony of fate, are suggested in these simple statements by a child. Although the situation is seen through a child's eyes and is expressed in the direct language of a child, it is nevertheless real and may well give pause to the flag wavers. This is a new approach to the frequently expressed idea that nobody really wins a war.

In the poem "Clouds" the intellectual contribution is the original imagery—original, at least, with the child who wrote it. It is not necessary that the idea be new to the world, but only that it be new to the child and expressed in his own way.

CLOUDS

Clouds
Are like a bouquet
Of white lilies,
And the blue sky
Is the vase.
–Wilbert Morris, age 11

Here is another poem in which a new idea—new, at least, to the young author—is expressed with delightful originality:

WHAT MAKES RAIN

When the clouds are black,
The angels wash them,
And that makes rain.
After that the sun comes out
And dries them,
And they are white again.
–Bessie Castro, age 12

The following poem also expresses a new idea:

MUSIC

Music
Is something inside of you
That sings.
–Timothy Hawkins, age 7

Perhaps the little boy who said that did not realize the profundity of his discovery. But when we study his verse, we see that he has stated what music actually is. We could not make music without that inner something that comes out as rhythm and melody. We could not hear music without that inner tuning and timing arrangement that helps us to distinguish and differentiate sounds. It is the "something inside of you" that we teachers are trying to awaken in our children, through poetry. It is the "something inside of you" that produces new ideas, original phrasing, fresh imagery. It is the "something inside of you" that makes the poet, as the writer of the following discovered.

A POET

A poet is not an ordinary person
Who gets poetry just from the sky or sun;
A poet is a person who gets his poetry
From the meaning in his heart.
–Edith Miller, age 15

We can expect to find intellectual contribution in the poetry of children, but we cannot urge children to make a conscious effort to put it there. We can encourage them to express themselves, and we can give them a chance to learn how poetry is made. We can search their poems for an original idea, a new approach to an old idea, fresh imagery, originality of phrasing, and especially, new insight (new, at least, to the child).

There is a type of poetry, which we may call the poetry of idea, that conveys to the mind of the reader an idea rather than an image. Although a poem of this sort may contain vivid imagery, its outstanding quality is the idea. Sometimes the idea approaches the philosophical; sometimes it deals frankly with fact. In the following poems the intellectual contribution is chiefly *idea,* expressed and elaborated upon. The first poem expresses a child's protest at the tendency of certain poets to dwell in the world of fancy and to ignore the world of reality.

MEET REALITY

Another world calls to you and me,
The tangible world of reality.
The millions tramping to and fro,
Millions out of work—where shall they go?
Are we just going to sit and gaze,
Or write about it, phrase by phrase?
–Mary Lois Heath, age 13

The next two poems complement each other, but both express the idea of the futility of hurry:

TUMBLEWEED

Man is like a tumbleweed
In a wind storm.
He is always rushing around,
But doesn't know where he is going.
–Wesley Johnstone, age 13

THE TURTLE

The poor little turtle
Walks so slow,
But he gets everywhere
He wants to go.
–Robert Tinsley, age 10

It may be that the writer of "Mussed Ball" was unconscious of the irony in his statement, but the idea is there for those whose experience makes it possible for them to see it:

MUSSED BALL

The world
Is a round ball
All mussed up.
–Gerald Glassman, age 11

The next poem sounds like a simple statement of grim fact; but the last line reveals the young author's insight, and it is full of implications for the mature reader.

WAR

Marching, marching onward,
Ten thousand onward going—
Each one a mother's son—
To the battle front grim and gray,
To shed their blood for another's quarrel.
—Olive Taylor, age 13

Inspirational poems are usually poems of idea. As a rule, such poems, especially if written by children, who are less skillful than are adults at pointing a moral, are likely to be prosy and insincere. Occasionally, however, as in the following, the excellence of the rhythm and the simple effectiveness of the phrasing more than balance the triteness of the optimism:

GRAY DAYS

When skies are gray and dreary,
Do not despair.
Though we cannot see the sun,
We know it's there.

The clouds will thin and break away,
One by one,
And there in all its glory
Is the sun!

So if your heart is dull and heavy,
Your trouble great,
Don't let your thoughts be gloomy;
Just wait.

The clouds of trouble will roll away,
One by one,
And happiness will shine again,
Just like the sun.
—Carol Lynn Fierke, age 13

Even the philosophical touch is found in the poetry of children:

OUTSIDE AND INSIDE

Inside's today,
Outside's tomorrow.
Somehow, some way,
I just can't say,
Inside's today,
Outside's tomorrow.
–Arthur Stasney, age 7

THE LIGHT OF KNOWLEDGE

A ray so dim
Gathers strength as it advances,
Becomes brighter and brighter,
Illuminates the darkness of stupidity,
Leaves in its brilliance
The knowledge of life,
And drives away once and for all
That ravaging thing, darkness.
–Jerry Rittenberg, age 13

The poetry of children may be as effective as that of adults in presenting ideas and truths that have made themselves evident to the young authors. We must encourage children to express their ideas picturesquely, by means of imagery and analogy, so that their efforts will not degenerate into jingly, moralistic verse. Such verse, unfortunately, is inclined to be pedestrian; it is the imagery that gives wings to poetry.

THE SUBJECT MATTER OF POETRY

Anything in life that is of value to individual or social development, anything that tends to help solve the riddle of existence, anything that leaves the reader satisfied at having shared a valid, significant, and universal experience, is proper subject matter for poetry. For poetry is not only the voice of the prophet crying in the wilderness; it is also the voice of the interpreter in a bedlam of strange tongues. The poet's mission is to find out what is going on and to interpret it to those who see but do not understand. The modern poet who spends his time among the stars, whose dreamlike existence touches not earth or the stuff of which life is made, is not accepting the challenge of his time. Willingness to face the problems of life and to try to interpret them, as well as the desire to discover the significance of common things, is the secret of the power of such poets as Chaucer, Shakespeare, Browning, Whitman, Frost, and Sandburg. Anything that is significant for life is significant for poetry.

As teachers of creative writing we are concerned specifically with the subject matter of poetry by children. We provide a creative environment and creative experiences for our classes in order to give them something to write about. We should not restrict the field; we must allow them liberty to express themselves naturally and sincerely about anything that touches their lives.

However, we must exercise guidance, for children exposed to out-of-school environments of all sorts often have entirely erroneous ideas of what constitutes poetry. We shall be obliged to discourage vulgarity, obscenity, personalities, clever superficiality, attempts to be funny, and nonsensical jingle, and to direct the choice of subject matter away from these byways of versification. In many cases, unfortunately, street-corner conversations, lewd picture cards, vapid advertising jingles, and misplaced praise for cleverness have already conditioned the youthful would-be poet before we get a chance at him. It is our task, then, to recondition him, to awaken his intellectual pride in real and serious creative effort.

The actual choice of subject must be left to the child, but we may call his attention to certain phases of life and seek to stir his response to specific experiences. In presenting poetry to children, we may find it effective to choose a subject beforehand and center all the inspirational activities about that subject. The subjects easiest to handle in this way are the simpler aspects of nature, the experiences common to the group, and the things by which they are surrounded. A collection of poems suitable to the age-group, alphabetically arranged by subject and filed in a looseleaf notebook, is an invaluable aid to the teacher engaged in creative writing activities. This collection should include not only the poems of well-known poets, but poems clipped from current magazines and the original poems of the children themselves.

Perhaps the most important part of this discussion of the subject matter of poetry by children has to do with what may be expected of children at different age levels. Their poetry should represent a natural unfolding and expansion of the personality; we should not apply a forcing process to induce them to produce verse too mature for their years. At the same time we must not allow them to remain on a lower level of maturity than their social and mental ages warrant.

SUBJECT-MATTER EXPECTANCY

The creation of poetry should not be reserved for any single period of a child's school life; it should be a growing and developing influence throughout his whole school career.

In the first and second grades the children will express their immediate, unreflecting reactions to objects, activities, and experiences. Their stories and poems will have narrative value rather than picturesqueness. They will talk about things they have made, things they have seen or done, pets and toys, and, with a little encouragement, the simpler aspects of nature.

In the poetry of children in the third and fourth grades picture-making begins to compete with narrative. The children may be taught to think of their little verses as word pictures, may consciously try to write word pictures that would help an artist in making a painting. Their poems will show expanding vocabularies, increasing skill in the use of words, and awareness of sensory impressions. They will be able to make simple analogies for things in nature, in their environment, and in the behavior of animals or of other children. In addition to immediate experiences, their subject matter will include remembered experiences.

In the fifth and sixth grades the children will be able to write about immediate experiences, remembered experiences, imagined experiences, objects in nature, ideas about the natural world, and simple emotional experiences. Their sense of imagery can be broadened by a study of imagery in poetry and a study of the various ways in which imagery is presented by poets. As their vocabularies expand

and their impressions of the world about them are deepened and multiplied, they will be able to find new and fresh images and analogies and to express them in original thought and phrasing.

The subject matter of the junior-high-school pupil shows awakening awareness of the beauty and the wonder of the world of nature, the complexity of the universe and of life, and the place of art in life. With his transition from the sixth grade he begins to change not his subject matter, but his approach to it. His awakening sensitiveness to external influences and impressions reveals to him hitherto unthought-of analogies. Ideas begin to creep into his poetry, ideas about relationships and the meanings of things.

The subject matter of senior-high-school poetry may be as broad as life and as deep as the maturity of the individual. The satisfactory expression of it will depend in part upon previous opportunities for creative experiences and creative expression, and in part upon the development of the student's own personality.

MEASURING SUBJECT MATTER AND STYLE

When I first began to encourage children to express themselves in poetry, a number of questions arose for which I had no answers. The most puzzling of these questions had to do with the quality of the product. Was the work of the children sufficiently mature for their age and grade? Were my standards of achievement high enough? Were they too high? How could I find out?

I set out to find the answers in the only way I knew. I gave the children in my charge many opportunities to express themselves freely and naturally without coercion, hampering criticism, or unfavorable comparisons. I studied and compared the work of children of various ages and in various grades until slowly but surely certain facts became plain to me and I was able to predict with some certainty the sort of creative writing that a given group would be likely to do. The standards that I have finally put into outline form are to be interpreted as indicating not what a child *ought* to do at a certain age or a certain grade-level, but what he *probably will* do if allowed to work freely without prodding.

Because of the fact that in the creative work of children the style is closely connected with the subject matter and is equally affected by the degree of maturity of the individual, I have included in the outline not only the subject matter most likely to engage the attention of the different age-groups, but also the style expectancy of each group. The teacher may use this outline as a sort of measuring stick by which he can determine whether or not he has made use of all the possibilities for his age group and whether or not his pupils are expressing themselves as well as they should for their age and grade. It is not, however, to be interpreted arbitrarily, for a sixth-grade child with the mental age of a fourth-grader will express himself like a fourth-grader. Children who are too young for their group, regardless of their mental ability, will often write poems that reflect not their mental maturity but their emotional age level.

Furthermore, there is the matter of previous experience (or the lack thereof) in creative writing. Junior-high-school boys and girls who have made no previous attempts to write poetry may, at first, turn in work on the fourth-grade level. They seem to begin at the beginning with immediate experiences and work through the successive phases until they reach their own maturity level. With consistent effort they frequently reach this level rather quickly. The teacher of older children should not feel discouraged when the first efforts of the class read like those of much younger children. Children will go through the stages of creative growth rapidly if they are given a little time, a chance to read and to hear good poetry, and many opportunities to write.

The expectancies mentioned in the following outline apply to normal children and not to prodigies or to children who have been especially conditioned to poetry. They are based upon my own forty years' experience with children of all ages, many of them from so-called underprivileged groups.

SUBJECT MATTER AND STYLE EXPECTANCY

I. First and second grades (ages 6 to 8)
    A. Subject matter: immediate experiences
    B. Style
        1. Largely narrative
        2. Little or no rhyme
II. Third and fourth grades (ages 8 to 10)
    A. Subject matter
        1. Immediate experiences
        2. Remembered experiences

- B. Style
  1. Narrative enhanced by picture words
  2. Simple analogies
  3. Little rhyme
  4. Occasional use of couplet and ballad stanza

III. Fifth and sixth grades (ages 10 to 12)

- A. Subject matter
  1. Immediate experiences
  2. Remembered experiences
  3. Imagined experiences
  4. Ideas about the natural world
- B. Style
  1. Falling off of narrative
  2. Expansion of picture-making quality
  3. Conscious use of analogy and imagery
  4. Use of simple verse forms and some rhyme
  5. Originality of thought and phrasing
  6. Sincerity of feeling but not depth of feeling

IV. Junior high school (grades 7, 8, and 9; ages 12 to 16)

- A. Subject matter (change of approach)
  1. Immediate, remembered, and imagined experiences
  2. Emotional experiences; deepening of feeling
  3. Ideas about the natural world
  4. Ideas about the relationships of people
  5. Ideas about self
  6. Beginning of the subjective approach to experience
- B. Style
  1. A groping for form and pattern, even in free verse
  2. First use of the vocabulary of emotion
  3. Occasional appearance of the longer poem
  4. The attempt to make a complete statement of the idea

V. Senior high school (grades 10, 11, 12; ages 15 to 18)

- A. Subject matter: as broad as life and as deep as the maturity of the individual
  1. Enrichment of emotional content
  2. Broadening of emotional perspective
  3. Awakening of interest in others and in the feelings of others
  4. Awakening of interest in world problems and in human problems
  5. Gradual formation of a philosophy of life

B. Style
   1. Use of various verse forms and patterns
   2. Indication of knowledge of and interest in simple rules and techniques of poetry
   3. Development of individuality in style
   4. Forceful use of imagery and analogy
   5. Appearance of symbolism
   6. Experimentation

6 Words for Poetry

THE POET'S WORDS

Like quicksilver balls
Poured from a shining vial,
They bounce in my thoughts.
–Marvin Lee, age 13

As an artist needs brushes and paints, as a violinist needs a fine violin, a poet needs words—vivid, colorful words, exciting words, vigorous words, words rich in emotional connotations. He searches for the right words not only to express his exact meaning, but also to arouse the imaginative, emotional, and intellectual response of the reader. He selects words that in sound and significance are appropriate to his theme, words that fit into the rhythmic pattern he has chosen.

The modern poet avoids old-fashioned poetic diction, flowery similes, and strained metaphor. He uses the direct, forceful language of today. But he selects his words carefully in order to produce conciseness, picturesqueness, exactness of meaning, and harmony of sound. He tries to make every word contribute something to the impact of his poem.

WORD CHOICE

The principal characteristics of an effective diction for poetry are simplicity, appropriateness, restraint, economy, and accuracy. When we say that the diction of poetry should be simple, we do not mean that the poet should never use a big word or an unusual word. We mean that his statements should be straightforward, should be readily understood by the reader, and should not be weighted down with artificial ornamentation, bewildering and unfamiliar allusions, and pedantic exhibitionism. The language of conversation is a good standard for the amateur poet. He must not let his search for beautiful, splendid, imaginative words lead him to adopt show-off words and artificial expressions that will cause his readers to laugh at his pretensions. He must say things in a straightforward way, simply and directly, as he would in conversation.

Ordinarily, younger children will tend to be simple and direct in their statements. But high-school pupils, especially if they have read much of the poetry of an earlier period, may fall into the error of unnatural adornment and involved expression. To them we must point out the value of simplicity as a qualification of good diction and a standard for modern poetry.

Appropriateness is the ability to say the right thing at the right time, to choose words that suit the mood, the emotion, the thought, and the rhythm. We can teach children to select appropriate words or phrases for their own poems by directing their attention to the quality of appropriateness in the poems they read.

Restraint gives added significance to diction and value to the poem. The tendency to tell all is often fatal to a poem; the best poems leave something to the imagination. In a description of war, for instance, gory details are likely to arouse in the reader a feeling of horror and disgust that carries over as a feeling of dislike for the poem. The poet who wants the reader to share his emotion and to agree with him must not use words and phrases that will have painful or disgusting associations. He must not resort to name-calling, which may antagonize, or indulge in personalities, which are always in poor taste. Violent language, vulgarity, and a tendency to "lay it on thick" weaken the verse in which they appear.

Whenever there are evidences of lack of restraint in the verses of children, we should point out that such expressions are in poor taste. The child whose work is not displayed with that of his classmates because of his use of words in poor taste will soon begin to exercise the necessary restraint. But the teacher should not go to the other extreme and emasculate the language. If poetry is to be of value as a force in modern living, it needs to use good, strong, red-blooded expressions that will support forcefully the truths it seeks to point out.

Economy is closely akin to restraint, except that it has to do with the numbers of words rather than with the kinds. Verbosity in poetry is no longer admired. Poets say what they have to say briefly and forcefully. Life moves so fast that there is no time for the long-winded poet who takes ten pages to expound an idea that could be well expressed in one; therefore, we are inclined to be critical of the poet whose work is full of careless repetitions, pointless digressions, and unnecessary sputterings. We teach our young poets to eliminate weak words, unnecessary words, and words that add nothing to the picture. We teach them to use words that mean exactly what they want to say and do not require additional phrases to explain them.

Accuracy in the use of words is just as important to the poet as to the lawyer. However, he achieves it not by adding all the words that could possibly be used in one connection, but by searching until he finds the *exact* word or phrase to express his meaning, a colorful word or phrase that fits into his pattern. The writing of poetry is one of the sure ways of promoting word study, and the result is bound to be an increased and more colorful vocabulary.

Good diction means not only accuracy of word choice, but also accuracy in word usage. Poems should be grammatically correct. Even very young poets can be taught to tolerate no inaccuracies in spelling, punctuation, or grammatical usage. For in so small a form as a poem such defects are very noticeable, and the young authors do not like the spotlight of criticism thrown upon their brain children.

In order to improve the quality of diction, one must understand the requirements of good diction and must practice; furthermore, one must eliminate archaic phrases, clichés, inversions, old-fashioned contractions, poeticisms, colloquialisms, and dated slang. We should teach children who may be intrigued by quaint words and phrases copied from their reading that words no longer used in writing or conversation are archaic and sound forced and insincere when used in poetry. We should show them that poor old worn-out words, like broken-down horses, are incapable of pulling their sky chariots along. The first words that come to mind are likely to be trite: "fleecy clouds," "gentle breeze," "wind and wave," "for you and me." The last phrase, usually included to finish a rhyme, is a cliché peculiar to poetry by children. We should encourage children to find newer, fresher words and not to be content with saying the same old thing in the same old way. Triteness is characteristic of mediocrity and comes from habit rather than from thought.

Inversions, because they are unnatural in the language, are not considered good form in the poetry of today. We do not say, "He climbed the hill high," or "He the door opened." Usually, such phrases are twisted about because of the need for a rhyme or because the author mistakenly thinks they sound poetic; actually, they are an admission of inexpertness in handling words.

For the same reasons, contractions out of general use should be avoided. We no longer say, "O'er," " 'twas," "ne'er," " 'twould," and the like; therefore we should not use such words in poetry. Furthermore, we should avoid such poeticisms as "morn," "eve," "beauteous," and "ere." These are the words of a past era, not in good usage in modern speech and writing, and therefore of no value in modern poetry.

And now a word about poetic license: It has been revoked. There was a period during which the poet claimed the right, under poetic license, to twist sentences by their tails, use words never found outside of poetry, and otherwise misuse the English language. But the modern poet feels that falling back upon poetic license is an admission of his lack of skill with words. Modern editors rarely accept poems in which poeticisms occur. We teachers must see that our young poets keep up with the fashions; anyway, since such expressions used by a child would be cribbed from his reading and would not be his own, they should be discarded on that account if on no other.

Except in dramatic poems in which people are talking, colloquialisms should be handled carefully because some are limited to one locality and may not be generally understood. Slang is to be avoided because it dates the poem, because it may not be universally understood, and because much of it is in poor taste and quickly becomes trite or goes out of fashion.

One way of salvaging trite words which are picturesque or essential to the poem is to use old words in new meanings. The poet who can turn an old word over and get a new meaning or a different perspective performs a real service to poetry. The word "sprinkling," in the following poem, illustrates such usage:

RAIN

Here is a little sprinkling
Coming down.
Now it is a great big rain.
Now it is big bubbles of water.
–Bobby Cash, age 5

The following poem contains a delightfully fresh usage of the word "bumps":

NEW MOON

The new moon bumps against soft clouds
As it sails across blue skies,
And bumping spills gay silvery dreams
To children with tight-shut eyes.
When night is done, the thrifty moon
Takes back the happy dreams.
He cleans them up with careful thoughts
And pours them out in streams.
–Mary Helen Sheller, age 8

Bees and blossoms have appeared in so many poems that they have become trite in combination. Yet the use of the word "honey-blossomed" lifts the following verse above triteness:

AIRPLANE

As I hear the roaring of the motor of a plane,
While it goes down its private cloudy lane,
I think of little bees as they buzz around,
Just above the honey-blossomed ground.
–Natalie Levy, age 12

The words in the next poem are not new or different or outstanding. They are all simple words that, taken alone, would not merit a second glance. But when the author makes the kite take a bow and makes the earth pull its tail, we have a new perspective on an old situation of kite flying.

THE KITE

A kite goes up
And takes a bow.
The earth pulls its tail,
And down it comes,
Wind-blown and torn.
—*Eulabell Hoff, age 10*

It is the poet's province, also, to coin words. Sometimes a poet who can not find just the right word to express his thought makes up one of his own. If it makes the thought perfectly clear so that everyone can understand it, the word may stand. Sometimes it becomes accepted as a word in good standing, sometimes not. Children often show a tendency to make up words. If the words fit the verses, are expressive and picturesque, why not accept them? Here are two examples of word-coinage:

STARS, GO AND HIDE

Stars, go and hide
Before the sun comes
To overfoam you.
Go hide
In your blue blankets
Up in the sky.
—*Teno Ruiz, age 13*

DARK NIGHT

The night
Is like a coal-black cat
That goes creaking over the trees
In the dark.
—*Lois Hicks, age 12*

The word "overfoam" is a coined word, but its significance is plain. The word "creaking" is found in the dictionary, but its usage in the poem is so startlingly different that it has all the effect of a coined word.

Of course, we shall not tell the children to make up words if they cannot find the words they need; but we must not discourage the use of the coined word if it adds to the effect of the poem.

Here is one last warning about the use of original poetry in the improvement of diction: keep as much as possible of the natural, childish expression. Correct only obvious errors in spelling and grammar. Point out clichés and poeticisms, but do not edit out everything that makes the child sound like a child. The delightful, fresh turns of word and phrase are just what we want. Children with their unspoiled eagerness should be able to add to the possibilities of diction; they should not be held down to dead, dry patterns of thought and modes of expression. Give them liberty—and watch poetry grow.

BUILDING A VOCABULARY

Our first task with respect to vocabulary building is to explore the everyday vocabulary of our students, asking ourselves such questions as these:

1. Are they making use of as many words as they should for their age and grade?
2. What sort of words are they adding to their lists?
3. Are they exposed to good writing in their textbooks?
4. Are they encouraged to read books that use picturesque, imaginative, significant language?
5. Are they making consistent attempts to increase their vocabularies?
6. Have we awakened their interest in words?

We must not overlook the fact that good writing in both prose and poetry is an essential part of the creative environment. We should never overlook an opportunity to point out good writing in any field of study and to call attention to the effective use of words and phrases to convey meaning and to arouse interest.

The next step is the encouragement of vocabulary improvement by the substitution of specific terms for the vague generalizations that beginning writers often use. Generalizations are usually dull and uninteresting. How much better it is to say, "The sunset was like a leaping flame" than to say, "The sunset was very beautiful." Children will enjoy a game in which they search for specific ways to state ordinary generalizations. The following examples may be helpful:

GENERALIZATIONS	SPECIFIC TERMS
There was a red bird in the woods.	A bird like a scarlet flame chased a grasshopper through the wild-cherry trees.
We sailed on a rough sea.	Crashing waves attacked the sides of our boat like battering rams.
Rain was falling.	Needles of rain stung my face.
At midnight the moon was shining.	The moon was like a great street lamp in the midnight sky.
The snow was soft.	The snow fluffed up like feathers around my feet.

Exercise

Make specific statements about each of the following:

A big tree	An odd-shaped rock	A strange appearance
A cloudy sky	A colorful pageant	A good result
A nice day	A beautiful vase	A pretty flower
A happy event	A pleasant experience	A lovely garden
A bad move	An inspiring view	A winter scene

The following lesson plan has been used effectively with groups in upper grades, in junior high school, and in senior high school.

THE WIND BLEW HARD

Divide the blackboard space into five columns. At the top of the second column write "The wind." Ask the group to think of other names for the wind, and write them in the second column.

Next, ask for adjectives to describe the various kinds of wind named, and write them in the first column.

In the third column write the word "blew," and ask for other words to substitute for it.

In the fourth column write the word "hard," and ask for more specific words to list under it.

In the fifth column write similes, using the word "like."

Ask the children to select what they like best from each column and compose one-sentence statements, as many as they can think of in ten or fifteen minutes.

The preceding exercise calls attention to the many ways of being specific about the wind. Some children may wish to use their statements as the bases of poems. Others will enjoy making a collection of poems about the wind. The following poems are suggested for reading aloud:

"Ode to the West Wind" by Percy Bysshe Shelley
"Do You Fear the Wind?" by Hamlin Garland
"The West Wind" by John Masefield
"Wind Song" by Carl Sandburg
"Wind and Silver" by Amy Lowell
"The Wind Tapped Like a Tired Man" by Emily Dickinson
"The Wind Took Up the Northern Things" by Emily Dickinson
"The Wind" by Robert Louis Stevenson
"Who Has Seen the Wind?" by Christina Rossetti
"Wind Horses" by Carl Sandburg
"To the Winter Wind" by John Gould Fletcher

Children may also increase their vocabularies by searching for and listing words which make specific appeals to each of the five senses.

Poems that demonstrate the use of concrete words and phrases will help to start creative imagination functioning, especially poems by other children who have learned to be specific. In each of the following poems every word helps to bring the picture into clear, sharp focus.

MY FRENCH DOLL

Azure and tan and silver is she,
Tall and graceful as a willow tree—
Silver clip and golden flower—
A Juliet for a modern bower.
–Marjorie Ann Miller, age 14

QUILT OF STARS

Stars are like stitches
On a quilt of blue,
Sewn by the darkness,
Washed in the dew.

The moon is the needle,
The Milky Way the thread
That sews the bright stars
Up over my head.
–Lorraine Moran, age 14

RECREATION!

Swing low, swing high, my sweet, lovely tree;
Let your vines swing with my music.
Let your leaves fall softly into the river,
To break the moon's beam on her back;
For she is tired after a hard rushing day.
Let us smooth her and make her happy.
–Maybelle On, age 14

RAIN

Blue rain is wetting and soaking the earth.
The patters sound beautiful at night.
Down the blue sky the raindrops slide
Like little elves having their fun.
–Charlie Dorado, age 15

TERMINAL ISLAND

Water splashes
Against the stained walls.
Fishnets lie
On salty decks.
Small boats swing,
Swaying with the waves.
The yellow people with squinting eyes,
On the boats,
Make ready,
Mending wet fishing nets
With tough white string.
–Jack Beckner, age 8

Here is a poem that shows the specific use of terms describing sound:

ARROYO SECO

Men working on the arroyo,
Crowded together,
Look like little cars moving around.
Their hand shovels sound like rhythm bands,
Tapping now and again the other shovels.
The big steam shovels,
With their deep-voiced motors,
Are the kettle drums
Keeping time to the beat of the orchestra.
The falling dirt
Sounds like the tonguing of horns.
The gravel and sand of the cement mixer
Are the deep, loud trumpets.
And tumbling out
Is the music of the band.
–Russell Blodgett, age 8

Another way to be specific is to use words that show action:

WIND

Trees in the wind
Wave in rhythmic time.
The wind makes the flowers sway.
The rolling leaves upon the walk
Dance till they fly far away.
And the roses swing their petals in time
To the brown-leaved orchestra.
–Iverna Lister, age 8

OUTWARD BOUND

Out into the bay she goes,
Plowing along.
The swells strike,
But nothing can stop her.
Yards strain.
The cry is, "All hands!"
Outward she goes–
She plows on and on.
–David Howard, age 10

SCARECROW

The tree
Is shaking like a scarecrow
Flapping his hands.
–Matsuo Hirose, age 10

THE DEER

Running as fast as he can goes the deer,
Always trying to catch up with the wind.
–Henry Renteria, age 15

DANCING WIND

Dance around me, little wind.
Pick the leaves
And dance with them,
Like a whirling top.
—Jessie H. Lopez, age 13

At the junior-high-school level children may be taught the relative values of the parts of speech in giving strength to an original poem. Verbs are the strongest because they give life and movement to the poem. Nouns come next because they stand for ideas, names, and things. Adverbs stand next to nouns in importance, and adjectives follow adverbs. Even though they describe, adjectives are less important than nouns because they have fewer connotations. Too many adjectives weaken rather than strengthen a line; they tend to confuse and blur the image. Prepositions are very important because they show relationships or distinctions. But connectives are relatively unimportant and should not be stressed. Here is a functional purpose for the study of the parts of speech: the necessity of determining their relative values for poetry.

The language of feeling is often used unconsciously by younger children; but children of junior high school age will know the sentimental terms in common use and will enjoy finding new ways of expressing the ordinary emotional concepts with which they are familiar. They should try to discover why some words are more poetic than others. They should search their favorite poems for words that suggest and imply as well as words that state, for words that set the mood, for words that have emotional associations. The words in the following poem set the mood:

LONELY TREE

A lonely tree on the desert
Looks like a sad person
Who is lost.
It stands there,
Strong, tall, and desolate.
—Esther Glasgow, age 12

There are emotional overtones for most readers in the words "lonely," "desert," "sad," "lost," "desolate." For instance, the word "lonely" calls to mind many other lonely things and places, as well as times when we ourselves have been lonely. This use of appropriate wording by a child, even though not consciously done, shows the truly poetic spirit at work. Emotional vocabulary helps to make the following poem, also, effective:

MY LITTLE CAT

My little cat sits all day long and purrs.
This morning, with bowed head, she knelt
Before my silent Buddha, as in prayer.
–Beatrice Howard, age 13

Other children have described cats. This child saw the cat only as an incident, and the cat's position as a symbol of some deeper significance, some inherent need to worship. Her use of words which for us have religious connotations—"bowed head," "knelt," "silent Buddha," "prayer"—adds emotional significance to an experience in observation and gives universal appeal to the verse.

The following poem achieves its purpose not by the words put in, but by the words left out. In two lines the poet has put squarely before the person who thinks it is grand to be a soldier the problem the soldier will have to face. It is stronger because there is no attempt to play upon the emotions of the reader by drawing a harrowing picture of the battlefield, and yet, the simple statement of fact couched in simple, straightforward language has a poignancy that is hard to forget.

LISTEN, SOLDIER

The time will come to use your gun:
You will kill a mother's son.
–Virginia Caspar, age 15

None of the poems quoted were teacher-taught. All three were spontaneous efforts, unrevised. All were the result of emotional reactions to experience. It is the poem that comes as the result of intellectual exercise rather than emotional experience that must be watched for incongruities of word and thought. The child who attempts to describe the emotion of another, an emotion that he has not yet felt, may overdo it. The child who is made too conscious of the emotionalized vocabulary is handicapped rather than helped; for his vocabulary will seem strained and unnatural and his poem insincere. We may point out in his poems word choices that are good and explain why they are good; but we should not put adult expressions into his lines nor insist that every little verse have emotional overtones. Instead of trying to drag out of the child what may not be there, we must wait and hope—and learn to recognize it when it comes.

POETIC SIGNIFICANCE

The language of poetry is the language of imagination, of beauty, and of feeling. The poet uses not only the significant, accurate word, but the word which at the same time presents the best picture and stirs in the reader an emotional appreciation of the poet's mood and idea.

Imagery, developed by the use of figures of speech, is the basis of the language of imagination. An image in poetry is a mental picture of an idea, presented in the terms of sensory appeals, of connotative language, of comparisons which help us to evaluate the unknown in terms of the known. When we express likenesses in objects that are in most respects quite different, we are making images. Since poetry communicates largely by suggestion rather than by direct statement, images help the poet to express his ideas of truth and beauty. To be effective, however, the images must be fresh and original.

A poet uses imagery to give concreteness to abstract ideas, to clarify in his own mind a thought or a feeling or a dim perception of truth, and to awaken in others a similar understanding and response. The imagery of a poem performs its true function when it helps to bridge the chasm between the poet and the reader.

Imagery includes comparisons, figurative language, concrete picture words, allusions, analogies, and sensory appeals of various types. It consists primarily of the expression of resemblances. The poet is constantly on the lookout for resemblances in things that are quite different. He finds resemblances in their inner nature or essence, in their qualities and characteristics, or in their activities; and he expresses the resemblances in simile or metaphor or some other figure of speech.

The following lesson plan, which begins the study of imagery in a somewhat more formal fashion than that presented in Chapter 2, has been used successfully in grades seven through twelve.

IMAGERY

An image is a mental picture of an idea. When you see and express likenesses in things that are really different, you are making images. This is an image:

Smoke is like a great gray feather.

When you put images into poems, you are using imagery. There are many kinds of imagery. The three most common types of images, called figures of speech, are the *simile,* the *metaphor,* and *personification.*

The simile: The word "simile" means an expressed similarity or likeness. The resemblance of one thing to another is stated. The word "like" is the sign of a simile. Sometimes, instead of "like," the words "as if" are used. These are similes:

The wind is roaring like a lion.
The bluejay shouted like a noisy politician.

The metaphor: The metaphor is more intensely poetical than the simile. A metaphor is an *implied* likeness. It speaks of one object in terms of another, or as if it were the other. These are metaphors:

The wind is a roaring lion.
Dry leaves are little brown kites riding the wind.

Personification: When a lifeless object is given the form or the characteristics of a living person, or behaves like a human being, the figure of speech is a personification. In the following sentence "night" is personified:

The full moon is the brooch with which Night fastens her blue velvet cloak.

Exercises

1. A simile consists of the name of the object being described, the name of the object it is said to be like, and the word used to express the likeness. In the following example the words in italics constitute the simile: The roaring *wind* is *like* an angry *lion.*

Copy the following sentences, and underline the words that constitute the similes:

The gently falling rain, like liquid diamonds, adorns the earth.
Clouds float in the blue sky, lazily, like swans on a still lake.
Airplanes roar like demons tearing through the sky to strike at their foes.
Men are like gods when silver airplanes give them wings.
The wind screamed about the old house like a banshee.

2. Write three original sentences containing similes, and underline the words which constitute the simile in each.

3. A metaphor consists of the name of the object being described, the name of the object it is said or implied to be, and the form of the verb "to be" that is used to complete the statement. Sometimes the verb does not appear in the metaphor. In the following examples, the words in italics constitute the metaphors: The *wind is* an angry *lion* roaring through the forest. When I look at the *stars,* I know why the poet said, "The night has a thousand *eyes.*"

Copy the following sentences, and underline the words that constitute the metaphor:

The clouds are fairy castles in the sky.
White moon, a great magnolia blossom, rests lightly on the hair of Night.
A blanket of snow covers the earth.
In the poem the lover called his sweetheart a rose and himself a thorn.
Misunderstanding, caused by angry words, was a wall between them.

4. Write three original sentences containing metaphors, and underline the words that constitute the metaphor in each.

5. Name the thing which is personified in each of the following sentences:

Sleep, lay your soothing hand upon my aching head.
Spring, with her basket of flowers, is dancing across the meadow.
When North Wind blows his icy breath across the pond, the children begin to sharpen their skates.
The ocean threatens with the voice of an angry giant.
The pages of my book speak to me with many voices.

6. Write three original sentences containing examples of personification.

After a specific lesson on images I read aloud poems that are outstanding for unusual or picturesque diction and imagery, asking the students to listen for a specific concrete word or phrase, a simile, a metaphor, or an example of personification in each. Such poems as the following are excellent for a lesson of this sort:

"Full Moon" by Sara Teasdale
"Dolphins in Blue Water" by Amy Lowell
"Night of Stars" by John Gould Fletcher
"The Mountains" by Hamlin Garland
"How the Waters Come Down at Lodore" by Robert Southey
"Wind across the Valley" by Raymond Holden
"Two Stars" by Melville Cane
"The Eagle" by Alfred, Lord Tennyson
"The Snow-Storm" by Ralph Waldo Emerson
"Look, Stranger, on This Island Now" by W. H. Auden
"The Bells" by Edgar Allan Poe
"Days" by Ralph Waldo Emerson
"The Cloud" by Percy Bysshe Shelley
"The Skylark" by Percy Bysshe Shelley
"Velvet Shoes" by Elinor Wylie
"Lost" by Carl Sandburg

When the children are ready to write, I encourage them to begin with the simplest of all figures of speech, the simile, and to try to put one simile into each poem. The following poems demonstrate the successful use of similes by children.

VIOLETS

Violets
Look like little blue pieces
Of plaster off the sky
Falling down
And changing into flowers.
They smell so clean and happy
It makes you think
That you are in a great big ocean
Full of perfume.
–Eva Ramos, age 12

CLOUDS

As I look up into the sky,
The clouds look like flowers
In heaven.
–Dolores Melendrez, age 10

RAIN

The rain is beating down
With a new fury,
And it seems to beat a tune
Like the drums of a savage tribe.
I can almost see their cold eyes
Gleaming in the darkness
Among the shadows.
It seems as if I were in a jungle
Full of savage life.
The rain is slowing down,
And now it makes a beautiful melody
Like distant bells
That are gently lulling me
To sleep.
–Faye Vaughan, age 13

RAINDROPS

Raindrops, raindrops,
Here come the raindrops
Like silver parachutes
Falling from 'planes.
–Ramiro Mercado, age 15

SNOWFLAKES

Snowflakes flutter down like butterflies,
Glistening silver in the sultry skies.
–Billie Wright, age 14

After they understand the simile, children may step up to the more difficult metaphor, with results such as these:

HOLLYWOOD VERSION

The moon is a searchlight in the sky,
Spotlighting the stars as they twinkle by.
–Mary Frances Beck, age 12

PEACE

Peace is a healing fluid
Flowing gently
From Mother Nature's golden urn of joy.
It quickly heals
The torn and bleeding hearts of men
The whole world over.
–Anne McPhee, age 14

POET MINER

A poet is but a miner of gold:
He searches through land and sea
To find the nuggets of loveliness
And the gold of poetry.
This miner must walk through rhythm gulch
To find the ore of rhyme;
He must take enough to make a ring
To the skillful blacksmith of time,
So that the blacksmith may make for him,
For the miner of poetry,
A magic ring of shining verse,
And a crown of memory.
–John Reed, age 11

SNOWFALL

Gently drifting feathers white,
All impinging on my sight
As they flutter from above—
Snowflakes, crystallized as love.
–Allen Taplin, age 13

Children can learn to recognize personification in the poems they read, but in their own work they are likely to use it less often than they use simile or metaphor. Occasionally, however, good examples of personification appear in such poems as the following:

UNWELCOME VISITOR

War has knocked upon our door.
  Shall we let him in
To clutter up our living room
  With death, disease, and sin?

Or shall we calmly call without,
  "Let your knocking cease.
The only one that we'll admit
  Is good old Mr. Peace."
    –Thelma Mackie, age 14

BUCKET OF STARS

Someone poured a bucket of stars
  Across the midnight sky.
They twinkled and smiled the whole night
    through
  Till Dawn with her broom swept by.
    –Sydney DeVore, age 15

PLEA FOR LIGHT

Mister Sky,
Won't you put on your light?
I'm such a small insect without light,
I'll soar into Mrs. Spider's net,
And Mrs. Spider is so sly!
So, Mister Sky,
Please put on your light,
So I can fly.
  –Gilbert Garcia, age 14

The language of imagination and the language of beauty are so closely interwoven that it is difficult to consider them as separate factors in poetic significance. For beauty feeds the imagination and is expressed in imaginative terms.

When we speak of beauty in relation to diction, however, we think not only of the beauty which the poet sees and tries to share through his poetry, but also of the intrinsic beauty of words and word sounds, and of patterns of thought. The poet becomes a true artist when he begins to give thought not only to the picture, but also to the frame. He examines his lines for harsh sounds and phrases unsuitable to the idea, and he substitutes for them sounds and phrases which are appropriate to mood and meaning. He selects words with accents properly placed to fit into the rhythmic pattern. He chooses euphonious words and makes intelligent use of alliteration, assonance, rhyme, and cadence. In this way he adds to the artistic significance of his work.

METHODS OF REVISION

Children should be encouraged never to regard one of their own compositions as finished, complete, and unchangeable. They should get into the habit of revising, of exchanging a weak word for a stronger word, of substituting more effective phrasing as they become more expert in the use of words. They should learn that constant revision of one's work shows growth in ability and in perception. The true artist in words is never satisfied with the stage he has reached; he wants to be more exact, more vivid, and more specific. Words being what they are, the ultimate perfection is never achieved, and so there is always incentive for improvement.

The critical evaluation of one's own poem should begin with the title. Even a child can learn that articles are not really needed and that they serve only to weaken the title. He can learn to recognize a title that is commonplace or that gives away the whole point of the poem, and to seek a better title. He can be taught to examine his poem for an interesting, unusual, or striking phrase, and to take his title from his most interesting words. The title for the following poem was chosen in this way.

TRADERS

The earth and sea are traders:
The sea brings sand to the earth
And the earth gives its tumbling, roaring rivers
To the sea.
–David Howard, age 9

"The Earth and the Sea" is a possible title and one likely to be chosen by the child. Omission of the articles will make it stronger: "Earth and Sea." But there is nothing outstanding about it. It doesn't express the real point of the poem. What is the significant word in the poem? "Traders," of course. It does not give away the whole idea, for we have to read the poem in order to find out who the traders are. There are dozens of poems about the earth and the sea. There will be few others, or none, called "Traders." Therefore, it is the best title, and the title that finally was used.

One's next task is to examine the lines for padding, for words and phrases that are not needed to make the idea clear. Such padding weakens the poem by lessening the compression and the intensity of the statement and by softening the impact. The first version of the following poem contains some padding, which is indicated by parentheses. These words add nothing to the picture or the meaning, and they spoil the rhythm. The omission of the padding makes a more effective poem with more rhythm, intensity, and impact.

(THE) FLOWERS

When you are sad (as can be),
(Lots of times) flowers can make you glad,
With their (many) shining little faces
All (turned) upright in the sun.

FLOWERS

When you are sad,
Flowers can make you glad,
With their shining little faces
All upright in the sun.
–Virginia Bridges, age 12

The third activity in the evaluation and revision of one's poem is the giving of attention to the sound quality of words. One of the best ways to teach children to use beautiful sounds is to let them read their poems aloud. Reading aloud helps them to select sounds that seem to fall into place naturally and to fit in with other sounds. If the poem flows smoothly and is easy to read, it will delight the ear. If harsh sounds are used, or broken rhythms, these will be detected in the reading, and changes can be made. Children can be taught the explosive effects of *b* and *p,* the musical effects of *l, r, m,* and *n,* and the hissing effect of too many *s*'s close together in a poem. They can learn how the use in one line of two or three words with the same initial sound (alliteration) enhances the beauty of the line, and they can search their favorite poems for alliteration. They will enjoy searching for words that are beautiful in sound as well as in meaning, and will try to add such words to their vocabularies.

7 ❧ Rhythms and Patterns

SILVER TREES

The silver trees are beautiful.
They stand so tall and still
They look like ghosts in uniform
Upon a frosty hill.
–John Sam Lewis, age 9

RHYTHM MAY BE INTERPRETED AS patterned sound, a regular recurrence of beat or swing produced by sound repeated at regular intervals. All language has rhythm. Unconscious but inevitable rhythm patterns are produced by the alternation of stressed and unstressed syllables, the rise and fall of the speaking voice, the division of sentences into natural phrase-groups, and the marking of intervals by pauses or by voice pitch.

In prose some intervals are longer than others, and they do not follow a regular pattern; therefore, we say that the rhythms of prose are irregular. Sometimes the rhythms are so irregular that they are difficult to detect; they seem to be accidental rather than deliberate. The writer of prose usually makes no effort to put rhythm into his lines. Such rhythm as appears is that inherent in the words and word-groupings.

Poetry, on the other hand, is highly selective. Conscious,

planned rhythm is one of its greatest assets. The pattern of stresses is definite and regular. Line lengths and meters are matched, and rhyme is introduced in order to enhance the rhythmic effect of the verses. The poet deliberately selects the more rhythmic word-groupings and chooses words which are in themselves euphonious.

TEACHING RHYTHM

I do not recommend going into the laws of versification with children. We should not make of poetry an exercise in scansion. No child needs to know the names of meters and of patterns in order to get rhythm into his own creative work. For rhythm is something that he feels rather than something he knows about. Rhythm is a natural manifestation of an emotional state, an expression of an emotional consciousness. When we speak of the teaching of rhythm, we refer to the guidance of a natural rhythmic sense to express itself in patterns recognizable as poetry.

Some teachers begin with rhythm, teaching the children to beat out rhythms before they have words to go with them and to create verses by fitting words to their rhythms. This approach, which is diametrically opposed to the method I have been advocating, is useful when the primary objective is the development of the sense of rhythm, and it can make effective use of marching rhythms, rhythm bands, rhythm exercises, and choral speaking.

When the objective is creative expression, however, one must begin with the imagination and allow absolute freedom in its development, touching upon matters of rhythm only after the child has acquired confidence in his ability to express his own thoughts and feelings artistically and imaginatively.

The true poems that children produce will have rhythm, even though we have not mentioned the subject of rhythm to them; for rhythm is one of the essential qualities of poetry, the one quality that distinguishes it from prose. The natural rhythmic sense of the child allows his creative work to fall into rhythmic patterns. When we read aloud to him, he hears the rhythm, and it is recorded in his mind. When he reads poems aloud for himself, he reproduces the rhythm, swaying his body or moving his head as he reads. When he listens to poetry, he frequently taps his fingers or his feet or marks the rhythm in some other way.

Rhythm is as natural to a child as breathing. He is born into a world of rhythm. When he bangs with his spoon or coos to himself, his noises fall into patterns of sound. As he grows, he mimics other sounds that attract him, over and over again, in little patterns. Playing by himself, after he learns to talk, he singsongs the things that he says, over and over. Children playing together make up little singsong games. They beat time with sticks and stamp with their feet, and the noises that they make fall into patterns of sound.

Unfortunately, much of our preschool training consists of suppressing the child's desire to make a noise. Instead of guiding his expressions into satisfactory channels, we hush him. By the time he arrives at school, he has learned to be still when he would much rather bang something to relieve emotional tension. If he enters a schoolroom that puts a premium upon silence and order (meaning quiet), his natural tendencies go still farther into hiding, so that by the time we get around to allowing him to express himself in ways we have selected, his inhibitions have erected barriers, and we must try to recondition his rhythmic sense.

Our approach will necessarily depend upon the age of the children and their previous experience, or lack of experience, with rhythm. Primary children should have their rhythm bands and their rhythm exercises. They should be allowed to discover and tap the rhythms in poems read by the teacher. They should learn their nursery rhymes and other verses with marked rhythms and have a jolly good time saying them.

But when they are seriously trying to put into words their own thoughts and feelings about an experience, they should not be urged to follow any certain rhythmic pattern. Insistence upon pattern will be likely to cause expression to degenerate into jingle. The emphasis should be placed upon the thought and upon the use of imagination; if the children have had plenty of experience in rhythm, the rhythms of poetry will come of themselves. Our goal is the natural child expressing himself in a natural way and in the rhythms natural to childhood. Many of the rhythmic patterns we try to force upon him are adult patterns or are not attuned to his personality; we should let him find his own.

Older children may give attention to kinds of rhythm, effects of rhythm, and rhyme patterns. They will enjoy reading and discussing poems in various kinds of rhythm. *The Poet's Craft,* by Daringer and Eaton, will be very useful in this study, for it presents poems arranged by rhythm groups, with a short explanation of the rhythm pattern of each. We should help children to see how rhythm is suited to the subject matter and the emotion of each poem, discussing with them line lengths, rhymes, and meters, beating out the time of each. If these facts are presented as bits of information that each child probably will want to know for himself, rather than as assignments on which the class is likely to be tested, the children will take an interest in them and will be likely to experiment with rhythms in their own poems. However, they must be left free to express themselves in their own way. Emphasis on rhythm rather than on imaginative expression may result in meaningless jingle.

DISTINGUISHING FREE VERSE FROM PROSE

Not every piece of unrhymed writing is free verse, even though it may be divided into short line lengths. Free verse has certain definite characteristics not possessed by prose, so that even if it is written out in prose form, it can be recognized as poetry. Teachers will find it essential to be able to make this distinction, for children, especially young children, often make no line divisions. In form their poetry is indistinguishable from their prose. Often they themselves do not recognize the poetic quality in what they have written.

The first of these characteristics is emotion. The difference between prose and poetry is chiefly the difference in emotional appeal. Poetry, arising out of emotion, expressed in the language of emotion, has a deeper emotional intensity than has prose. Every word enhances the emotional effect; every line speaks directly to the heart of the reader. The language of emotion tends to be a rhythmic language. The greater the emotion, or the greater its intensity, the more rhythmical is its expression. Consequently, even in free verse the rhythm is more noticeable than it is in prose.

The poetry of children will not be deeply emotional, but it will be sincere and vital. Because of the fact that the child is trying to express an emotional experience, his writing will fall into cadences that can be marked off as free-verse lines. If he is merely describing something he has seen, his writing is likely to be prose, regardless of the way he arranges the lines; but when he begins to be subjective, to put into his work something of his own intimate feeling, he begins to speak in poetry, and the difference is easily discerned.

The following poems illustrate this point. No matter how they are written, whether as paragraphs or as poems, they fall into certain distinct cadences when read aloud and thereby prove themselves to be true poems.

SILENCE

Motionless I stand.
My breath is heavy and slow,
My heart beating with the earth's rotation.
Like the smoldering, fiery depths beneath,
My eyes sting and smart.
Statue-still, I do not move
For fear of shattering the spell
Of eternal silence.

–*Constance Johnston, age 14*

POWER

Suns, planets, meteors,
All whirling,
Go forward across the heavens
At a terrific pace,
Through endless millions of miles.
The earth—
One little grain of dust
In this endless universe.
How could it be anything but inconspicuous
To the great Creator of it all?
One man lives,
Comes into power for a day,
Dies,
Is forgotten.
Men fight to gain power—
Power over what?
A little grain of dust.

–*Virginia Wheatley, age 13*

Although the fundamental distinction between free verse and prose is the difference in emotional intensity, there are other distinguishing characteristics that must not be overlooked. One of these is diction. The difference lies not in the kind of diction, but in the way words are used. Free verse has a greater economy of diction than prose, and it admits of less padding. The goal of the writer of free verse is to find the exact words to express his meaning, to choose significant, forceful words, and to make sharp, clear-cut, definite images. The idea must be expressed accurately and concretely in terms of beauty. Since the poet has discarded rhyme and meter, he must emphasize the imaginative quality of words and word-groupings, if his verse is to stand as poetry.

The following poems illustrate economy of diction, concreteness, and excellent imagery. Every line adds to the picture and helps to produce a completeness of effect. There is no padding and there is no vagueness.

THE JUNGLE

Lions crawl through tall grass.
Leopards like striped blankets
Sleep on the sun-beaten rocks.
Monkeys swing from mossy trees.
Antelope bounce down thin paths,
And hot winds flicker through thick bushes.
–Claire Gilbert, age 9

WINTER NIGHTS

On cold winter nights
Icicles hang from rooftops.
Beneath the fallen stars,
They glitter in the moonlight
Like shadowed glass.
The winds blow the trees,
Heavy laden with snow.
The icicles tinkle
Like silver bells.
–Douglas Qua, age 8

Tone color is also more important in free verse than in prose. The expert uses all the devices of sound—alliteration, assonance, onomatopoeia, and the like—to strengthen and beautify his phrases and his effects. Children can be taught to recognize alliteration and to use it sparingly, and occasionally to find words that resemble the sounds they are describing. But usually tone color in the poetry of children will be accidental rather than intentional. And yet, it is surprising how often effective combinations do appear in their poems. When the poetic spirit is at work, when the child is trying sincerely to express his own thought and feeling, imaginatively and artistically, he often instinctively selects the most appropriate phrases and sound combinations. The alliteration of the *s* and *w* sounds in the following poem brings out the whispering idea and gives the actual effect of whispering.

SUMMER WIND

Breath of a dragon,
Whispering round my window—
The soft summer wind.
—Barbara Johnson, age 13

In the next poem the alliteration of explosive *b*'s in the last line produces the suddenness of bursting bubbles.

BUBBLES

Transparent worlds
Floating in the summer air,
Bursting in the breeze.
—Shirley Roth, age 13

In the next poem the young poet tried to describe the sound and to tell what it made her think of. She also tried to reproduce the actual sound she heard as she held the seashell to her ear. I have tried to spell phonetically what she said.

SHELL SONG

The sea shell
Sings a song
In your ears
About rivers
Going in and out,
Singing
Sshuu—sshuuu!
–Beatrice Lopez, age 8

Perhaps we may think of free verse as concentrated prose. Although it is more highly emotionalized and uses a more selective diction, it has borrowed the rhythms of prose. It is like prose in that it moves by cadences rather than by metrical feet. It has an organic rather than an artificial rhythm; that is, as the thought and the emotion change from one line to another, the rhythm makes corresponding changes. The rhythm depends upon the sense and the emotion of the cadences. The arbitrary line division, therefore, is not the right sort of division for free verse; prose divided into short lengths lacks organic rhythm. Each cadence should have a special part in the development of the idea and the expression of the emotion.

The proper phrasing of free verse (that is, line division) helps the reader to feel the organic rhythm. One should put together in a line those words that seem to belong together in sense and in sound, not chopping off a line in the middle of such a phrase. The following verse is incorrectly phrased:

MONTEREY COAST

Mighty arms of
Land stretch out over the
Quiet Pacific,
While waves lap at
The foot of the matted
Hills of pine, leaving
White spun-lace
Clinging to the
Root-held land.

Reading aloud, making a slight pause at the end of each line, will show what is wrong with the phrasing. The words "Mighty arms of land" belong together and should not be separated. The poem is awkward and jerky. It lacks rhythm when it is read according to the line divisions, and the broken cadences irritate rather than please the reader. Free verse should be printed and read in units of meaning rather than in units of measure, as in the following corrected version:

MONTEREY COAST

Mighty arms of land
Stretch out over the quiet Pacific,
While waves lap at the foot
Of the matted hills of pine,
Leaving white spun-lace
Clinging to the root-held land.
–Constance Johnston, age 13

The best way to determine whether or not a given poem has rhythm is to read it aloud. The ear can determine as the eye cannot any jerkiness or unevenness. In checking rhythm, one should listen to the sound value rather than to the sense. The intervals will be marked by pauses and by voice pitch, which will indicate proper places for line divisions.

In making line divisions in free verse, one should not make all lines the same length. Variety in the length of line strengthens the poem by preventing monotony. Lines that have the same syllable length will sound like a poor imitation of meter. If the thought rises to a climax, it is sometimes a good idea to begin with long lines and end with short lines, as in the following:

MOON ON THE WATER

The laughing moon with silver moonbeams
Comes dancing on the lake.
They look to me
As if I could reach out and take a moon ray
And lock it in my heart.
–Katherine Schickel, age 12

FIRE FOXES

The young red foxes
Leap out at me
And up the chimney,
Flashing
Their lightning brushes
Of flame.
–Lucia Alice Cheyney, age 9

It is equally effective to begin with short lines and end with long lines, as in the following:

STARS

The stars
Are like little colored birds
That follow me wherever I go.
–Joyce Lauricella, age 7

LIGHTS

At night
Lights shining on our street
Look like yellow topazes.
Lights sparkling on the steps
Are flowing waterfalls.
And from the windows of the houses
Light flares like glowing fire.
–Vivian Anderson, age 9

Such arrangements make the reader feel that the poem is planned and is not just the haphazard expression of a lazy person.

If there is a sudden change in the thought, it may be indicated by a change in the rhythm. This device serves to emphasize the thought. Since each line of free verse should consume the same amount of time in the reading, variety is obtained and emphasis is provided for by the difference in line lengths. A short line must be read more slowly, and so receives greater stress. A long line speeds up the movement and is excellent for rollicking effects or for quick action. In the following poem the short first line, read slowly, gives us the feeling of the stillness and immovability of the rock walls. In order to give the succeeding lines the same time intervals as the first, it is necessary to read them more quickly; and this speeding up produces just the effect of rushing water that is needed to make the poem successful.

PALM SPRINGS

Brown rock walls
Hold the swift running water.
Palm trees with big green leaves
Hanging over the splashing creek
Color the bouncing stream
As it foams above smooth wet rocks.
—*Jack Beckner, age 8*

It is probable that the child had no conscious knowledge of this principle of free verse; but because his emotional experience was authentic, and because he was sincerely attempting to express his own thoughts and feelings, his poem shows the truly poetic spirit at work. Real poetry comes by inspiration rather than by intention; that is, it comes from the emotional rather than from the intellectual center.

Although some free verse poems contain casual rhymes, it is usually wiser not to mix free verse with rhyme or meter. The mixture seems to indicate the amateur and is likely to weaken the poem by calling attention from the thought to the form. If the writer starts with free verse, he should stick to free verse to the end of the poem and should not introduce rhyme or meter into any of the lines. If he starts with rhyme and meter, he should carry out the pattern all the way through the poem. Children can be taught this much of patterning without hindrance to freedom of expression. They can be taught to remove casual, unpatterned rhymes, when they can do so without detracting from the ideas they are trying to express.

PATTERNS FOR POETRY

Primary children need not be told anything about verse forms; they can have fun finding images for things and sharing their experiences by making word pictures. Some of them will speak in couplets, in tercets, or in quatrains, probably by imitation, but most of them will speak naturally in little free verse rhythms, unless the teacher consciously tries to shape or direct their thought. It is wiser not to attempt such direction. Absolute freedom in form, in subject matter, and in expression is essential to the true expression of creative imagination. The children should be themselves.

Simple forms may be taught to children at the junior-high-school level, and possibly even to fifth- and sixth-grade children who have already done some work in free verse. They should not be presented until the children have overcome their first inhibitions toward self-expression in poetry and are writing naturally and without restraint. Then they may be presented one at a time, not as lessons that *must* be done, but as new and interesting experiments. The children should look into volumes of poetry for examples of the forms being studied, and they should work out a few together, as a class exercise. Each of them might try to rewrite in the desired form a free verse poem of his own.

If the verse forms are presented before the children have learned to work easily and freely in the medium of verse, they may discourage effort and reduce the quality of the work produced. The important thing is that children have ideas to express and that they express them in the language of poetry. A feeling for form will be developed as they mature.

UNRHYMED VERSE FORMS

One unrhymed verse form which children enjoy is the *haiku,* a seventeen-syllable verse of Japanese origin. In English it is written in three lines based upon a syllable count of 5-7-5. That is, the first line has five syllables, the second line has seven syllables, and the third line has five syllables. Sometimes called an atmosphere poem, it is also a poem of mood and of symbolism. It may be solemn or light, serious or gay, religious, satirical, or even humorous. It may be as delicately charming as a dragonfly's wing or as deep-toned as a temple bell. But whatever its mood, it must fullfill certain requirements if it is to be a true *haiku.*

To begin with, it must have poetic significance. Any seventeen-syllable statement of fact, or of thought based upon observation or philosophical perception, may be divided into three lines of 5-7-5 syllables. But only those statements that suggest more than they say, that record inspired moments in clear-cut pictures, that present an emotion symbolically in a frame of beauty definitely calculated to arouse an emotional response in the reader are true poetry.

Another requirement of the *haiku* is the use of both the general and the specific term. Sometimes the general term is in the title, which is illustrated or explained by a specific instance that constitutes the poem, as in the following:

MYSTERY

The moss of the South:
A mysterious damp veil
Hiding the future.
–Helen Heyden, age 12

CONTRAST

The blue autumn sky
Shifts to a radiant red—
Then the black of night.
–Shirley Harmon, age 14

PROGRESS

Roaring through the blue,
Silver streak from coast to coast,
Mighty airliner.
–Tom Splender, age 14

Sometimes the title is the specific term, and the universal application is found in the poem. The following *haiku* illustrate the use of the specific term in the title and the general term in the poem:

CANDLE

Birth is a candle.
Childhood is a blush of light.
Death is melted tallow.
–Constance Johnston, age 13

VALENTINE GREETINGS

Gold dust in the sky,
Lacy clouds that dip about—
Nature's valentine.
–*Kathryn L. Sexton, age 14*

The *haiku* must also have seasonal significance. There must be in it some word or expression to indicate the time of year, in order to form a setting for the picture which the poet is trying to project upon the reader's mind. The season may be mentioned in the title or in one of the lines, or indicated symbolically, as in the use of snow to suggest winter. There must be in the *haiku* a definite reference to nature. To the Japanese all manifestations of nature are symbolical and have traditional significance. Every Japanese poet and reader knows what the symbols are, and therefore the simplest phrases may be packed full of meaning.

In addition to seasonal significance and nature symbolism, the *haiku* must have emotional significance. It must combine the objective view of nature with the poet's subjective approach to the expression of an experience. The poet's use of season must be symbolical of his feeling, mood, or emotional experience. And he must express this intimate personal feeling in terms of nature.

We shall not, of course, confuse children with so much detail. But it is well for the teacher to understand the form before trying to teach it. The teacher needs to know the principles of *haiku* in order to be able to evaluate the efforts of children. By the use of many examples, the children may become familiar with the 5-7-5 syllable count. They may learn that *haiku* are nature poems usually mentioning the season and telling or suggesting or implying the poet's feeling about something. They may examine Japanese prints and learn that the *haiku* is to poetry as the Japanese print is to art. They may write out their ideas in free verse form and then attempt to rewrite them as *haiku*. They will enjoy studying the following *haiku* to see how well the author of each has observed the rules of syllable count, mention of nature, and reference to season.

PAINTED SHADOWS

Trees stand strangely still
At twilight, painted shadows
Of their daytime selves.

–Jack Green, age 12

ON THE PIER

Before the sunrise,
For the fisherman waiting
The wind has shark teeth.

–Leslie H. Walter, Jr., age 14

WINTER WIND

A strong winter wind
Is like a lion roaring
In a great jungle.

–Beatrix Morgan, age 15

LOVELY LADY

Her feet fall like snow
As she walks in the garden
Saying a prayer.

–Beverly Wilson, age 12

RAINDROPS

Raindrops are lonely—
They come to earth to visit,
But we close our doors.

–Jack Klepper, age 13

TIME

Time is to the young
Like a turtle creeping by,
To the old, a deer.

–Juanita King, age 13

Writers who are seriously trying to adapt the *haiku* to the English language are beginning to feel that it should be as grammatically correct as any other poetic form in English. Omissions that make awkward constructions, as well as line endings that break the cadence, are amateurish and inexpert. For example:

JANUARY SUNSET

Dying fire in West	5
Love persistent in cold of	7
Winter's white silence.	5

Neither the thought nor the grammatical construction is clear. A colon after *West,* to take the place of the missing verb, would help to clarify the meaning. It is not customary in English, however, to omit the articles in order to make the syllable count come out right, and the reader becomes conscious of the missing articles before *West* and *cold.* Any distortion of language in order to make the thought fit the pattern is not skillful writing. The second line, awkwardly ending in a preposition, further advertises the writer's lack of skill.

The statement should be not only grammatically correct, but also poetically correct. The grammatical construction might be straightened out as follows:

JANUARY SUNSET

The dying fire is	5
Love in the coldness of the	7
Winter's white silence.	5

In other types of poetry in English, ending a line with "is" or "the" is definitely inexpert. It is generally understood that cadences must not be broken by line endings. Since the *haiku* written in English is an adaptation of an Oriental form to our language, it should follow the rules of English in its construction. Properly cadenced, the verse would read as follows:

The dying fire	4
Is love in the coldness	6
Of the winter's white silence.	7

But then the syllable count is no longer 5-7-5, and the result is not *haiku.* Further study may produce the following arrangement:

JANUARY SUNSET

Dying western fire	5
Is love defying coldness	7
In a white silence.	5

Here the cadences and the line endings coincide; each line ends on a strong word, and the syllable count is 5-7-5. The poem has been made grammatically correct, is poetically satisfactory, and is much strengthened by the rearrangement of the lines and the omission of unnecessary words. One technical criticism of the foregoing verse may be made with respect to the internal rhyming of *dying* with *defying. Haiku* should have neither end rhyme nor internal rhyme.

Many so-called *haiku* do not contain a reference to season. The Japanese have another name for such bits of verse—*Senryu* (pronounced "sendroo" with no accent and very little emphasis on the *r*). The *Senryu* was named for the Japanese poet who invented it. It may be about anything, but because it lacks the nature symbolism and seasonal reference, it is considered much less artistic than the *haiku.* Nevertheless, it may be counted as poetry if it has a significant idea and a poetic image.

With American and English writers the *haiku* is just an experiment in verse form, a pleasant little exercise to stimulate imagination and improve skill in word choice and usage. But in Japan *haiku* is a serious art, and the reading and writing of *haiku* have become increasingly important. From the very beginning of their school lives, boys and girls in Japan are taught to feel, to read, and to compose *haiku.* There is a *haiku* club in almost every town, even to the smallest village. Many *haiku* magazines are published, and there are frequent newspaper *haiku* contests. The older schools of thought have many followers; but just as in English, there are some writers who scarcely distinguish between poetry and prose. Genuineness and originality, however, are the standards for all.

The value of the study of *haiku* to English-speaking students and writers lies in its influence upon the development of the powers of imagination and upon writing skill. The necessity for conciseness encourages care and exactness in word choice and usage. One who is obliged to make a single significant detail represent a multiplicity and complexity of associated ideas must exercise the highest degree of imagination and skill, if his poem is to stand as the complete expression of a creative experience.

The *tanka* is also a Japanese form; it is the *haiku* with two lines added—or perhaps it is more accurate to say that the *haiku* is the *tanka* with the last two lines dropped. For in Japan the *tanka,* once popular, has decreased in popularity as the *haiku* has come more and more into favor. At one time the *haiku* was thought of as a man's poem, whereas the *tanka* was a woman's poem; but this distinction has not been rigidly maintained. The *tanka* consists of thirty-one syllables arranged in five lines based on a syllable count of 5-7-5-7-7. That is, the first and third lines are five syllables long, and the second, fourth, and fifth lines have seven syllables each. Rhyme and meter are not used. Simplicity, reference to nature, and good grammatical structure are desirable in the construction of the *tanka* in English. The following poem is an example of this form.

PEACE IN THE GARDEN

Footprints in the snow,
Side by side, the large and small,
Across the garden,
Show me that my dog and cat
Have forgotten their feuding.
–Elna Smith, age 15

The cinquain, an unrhymed verse form invented by Adelaide Crapsey, is, like the *haiku,* an atmosphere poem. It suggests rather than explains, and it uses nature references to indicate emotional states. The form, as its name suggests, consists of five lines based on a syllable count of 2-4-6-8-2. Rhyme is not used, and metrical regularity is avoided. In the writing of the cinquain, it is good practice to make the line endings and the cadences coincide, so that there will be no jerkiness or displeasing effect. The following verse illustrates the technique of the cinquain:

BEGGARS

Poppies
Hold up their cups,
Like beggars, to the sun,
Hoping that he will fill them full
Of light.
–Jane Hanson, age 14

These three unrhymed verse forms have found general acceptance, are simple and easy to present, and will usually satisfy the desire of the high-school boy or girl who wishes to pattern unrhymed verse. In teaching these forms, one should insist that the poet first write out his idea and decide upon his image before he tries to fit his poem to the mold, so that the finished product will not be just an empty form.

SIMPLE RHYMED VERSE FORMS

In rhymed verse the easiest and simplest form, of course, is the couplet. The end words of the two lines should rhyme, and the syllable count of each line should be the same. The couplet may be long or short, and it may follow any metrical pattern. When the couplet stands alone as a poem, it must show creative imagination, give the feeling of completeness, and have artistic significance.

Children should practice making single couplets before they attempt longer poems in the couplet form. They may play rhyming games until they know the difference between true rhymes and near rhymes. They may learn how to count syllables and how to beat out the time of their lines so that both lines of a couplet will be of the same length. The following verses show what interesting use may be made of the single couplet:

THE RED-WINGED BLACKBIRD

With his red-tipped wings outlined with yellow,
The red-winged blackbird's a handsome fellow.
–Lois Faye Gillette, age 10

WIND

The wind bends the trees to the very ground,
And then snaps them back with a swishing sound.
–Peter Rankin, age 12

STAR

When I see a star in the sky
I seem to look you in the eye.
–Elmer Logan, age 11

The tercet, also called the triplet, is less common but is fun to try. Any poem of three lines is a tercet, whether rhymed or not; but the tercet with each line ending in the same rhyme sound is the most artistic form. As in the couplet, the end rhymes should be true rhymes, and the line lengths should be the same. The mood of the tercet is one of lightness and grace. It is not suitable for sad or tragic themes. The following verses illustrate the use of the tercet:

FIRE AT NIGHT

Look at the fire at night:
It looks like a dragon fight
There in the blazing firelight.
–Carlton Robinson, age 12

NIGHT'S JEWELS

The stars are high and white,
The thin new moon is bright:
Gems in the hair of night.
–Bob Johnson, age 13

The quatrain is the most popular of the short verse forms. It consists of four lines in any rhythm; however, the rhythm should be consistent throughout any one quatrain. That is, if iambic pentameter is chosen for one line, the corresponding line should also be in iambic pentameter. Several rhyme schemes are possible: *a a b b, a b c b, a b b a, a b a b.* The last form, rhyming *a b a b,* is the most skillful and complete, and is acceptable for adult poetry as well as for children's poetry. The other three are, by adult standards, less skillful; they give the impression of being incomplete as single poems, even though some good poetry has appeared in these forms. However, the *a b c b* and *a a b b* forms are easy for children and are acceptable from them if the rules of rhyming and of matched line lengths are observed.

The child should be encouraged to write out his ideas first in free verse form and to decide upon the images he wishes to use. Then he should beat out the rhythms of several quatrains in varying line lengths until he finds the one he thinks suitable for his poem. He should choose end words for which rhymes can easily be found. Finally, he should try to put his poem into quatrain form without destroying the idea or losing the image. The following examples will show what sort of success with quatrains may be expected from children:

SURGEON'S HANDS

His hands are swift,
    His hands are sure;
He has the gift
    To heal and cure.
        –Don Russell, age 12

DESERTED HOUSE

Abandoned? Yes, forsaken and dark,
    The dreary home of ghosts.
The dusty cobwebs are the mark
    Of horrid, ghastly hosts!
        –Richard Burgess, age 13

SWANS

The beautiful white-feathered swans
    Are swimming on the blue-green lake.
The fairies with their star-tipped wands
    Are floating in their wake.
    –Margaret A. Compton, age 12

MISCHIEVOUS WIND

The wind goes dancing all about;
The wind has fun, without a doubt.
There go the leaves I had in a pile;
The wind is in mischief all the while.
    –Gordon Stromme, age 12

RAIN

The clouds are really little bowls
That hold the rain away up high.
The lightning comes and breaks the clouds,
And the rain comes dripping from the sky.
    –Marilyn Rayburn, age 12

WAVES

The waves came splashing upon the sands,
From far away countries and foreign lands.
The foam on the waves whitewashed the shore,
And the water hit with a great big roar.
    –Vernon Sewards, age 15

PEACE

The souls of men are tired of war;
    Their hearts cry out for peace.
God grant the time will soon be here
    When thoughts of war will cease.
        –Carol Lynne Fierke, age 13

DEVIL WIND

The wind is a devil
  That creeps to your door
And blows the rugs
  Right off the floor.
    –Charles Parchman, age 12

AFTER THE RAIN

I love to watch the puddles
  Before they start to dry.
They look quite small and shallow,
  But they hold the trees and sky.
    –Keith Woodward, age 11

SNOW AT CHRISTMAS

Christmas is coming;
  Pine trees will grow
White with beautiful
  Lily-white snow.
    –Charlotte Siegel, age 12

SOUND OF THE SEA

What is that noise that sounds afar?
  We listen in deep wonder.
It sounds like the roar of a lion,
  And the pounding hoof of thunder.
    –David Vasquez, age 14

The *a b c b* and *a a b b* forms of the quatrain are less complete in effect than the *a b a b* form, but each of them may be improved by the addition of a couplet to make a six-line poem. The six-line poem appears with varying rhyme schemes. Children who try this form must make sure that corresponding lines have the same syllable length and that their rhymes are true. The same technique as that used in developing the quatrain may be used in developing the six-line poem. The following examples of the six-line poem show what children can do with the pattern:

BUSY BOAT

My little boat goes sailing
On a rainy day.
I know it doesn't like it,
But it has to go away.
It meets the other boats
But cannot stop to play.
–Doris Nastase, age 7

MID-WINTER DREAM

I sat by the window one winter day
And idly watched the snowflakes play.
Each flake seemed to be a fairy hat
Tossed down to me—think of that!
I wondered where they hurried to,
When they tossed their hats and away they flew.
–Frances Schweitzer, age 13

FANCY'S STEED

Poets are blessed by a wonderful horse
Driving their visions ahead.
Pegasus flies far across Fancy's land
Up to a star-filled bed!
But he never finds time to rest, it seems;
For he keeps busy kicking down star-dust dreams.
–Vanda Lehman, age 15

WORLD ALWAYS NEW

Oh world so full of lovely things—
Flowers, birds with gaudy wings,
Tall old trees to give us shade,
Bright sunsets that never fade—
You are so old, and yet so young
You prattle with a childish tongue.
–Harold Wingate, age 12

LOVELINESS

Old mission, how I love you,
With your bells so sweet and clear;
Old mission bells, old mission bells,
You echo through the air;
Old mission bells, old mission bells,
Your tones are like a prayer.
–Lois Prante, age 9

SPRING-TIME SNOW

Spring-time snow is petal-soft,
And smells divinely sweet
Of hyacinth and trillium,
Of crocus shy and fleet.
It falls on woods and gardens,
But never on the street.
–Jill Douglas, age 14

Usually, children cannot sustain a thought through a long poem. Even in the commonest of the longer forms, the eight-line poem of two four-line stanzas, they are likely to repeat themselves. All that the poet has to say is usually said in the first stanza. And yet, there are children who do occasionally produce splendid longer poems. The teacher should teach the shorter forms and present examples of the shorter forms for study, but should give careful reading to any longer poems which may be turned in and individual help to the child who needs to eliminate repetitions.

High-school boys and girls, of course, are capable of longer poems, but the majority of them still find greatest success with the short forms. Only those whose deep interest is in writing should be encouraged to work out the more intricate patterns of poetry.

There are, however, exceptions to every rule. Children do occasionally produce successful long poems such as the following. But we must remember that these are exceptions; perhaps once in a semester a teacher will get a poem of this sort from a younger group.

HOW MANY THINGS ARE BRIGHT

The sun is bright,
The moon is bright,
The stars are bright,
And I am bright.
I can think of things you can't.

The sun is bright,
The moon is bright,
The stars are bright,
And you are bright.
You can think of things I can't.

The sun is bright,
The moon is bright,
The stars are bright,
And we are bright.

–William David Walter, age 8

CASTLES IN THE CLOUDS

Great white fluffy clouds,
Like castles in the sky:
Some are little, some are big,
And some go drifting by.

Some are the castles of Dukes,
Some are the castles of Kings,
And one is a funny little castle
That belongs to a girl who sings.

Some are the castles of Knights,
Some are the castles of Earls,
And one is the castle of robbers
Who stole her necklace of pearls.

One castle has a round tower,
One has a very large bell;
But which is the castle of the girl who sings,
I'm sure I cannot tell.

–Ernestine Mueller, age 10

THE NILE

Listen, you artists, listen;
I'll paint you a picture, too,
Of the tall and graceful palm trees,
And the Nile so rich and blue.

In the summer it floods the valley,
In the winter, recedes once more.
No, this is not a riddle—
It's the Nile with its winding shore.

And towering high in the heavens,
Above sand and temples, too,
We see the graceful palm trees
Outlined against the blue.
–Kathryn Akins, age 14

THE STUFF OF DREAMS

Down through the rose and the gray of the heavens,
Out of the sleep of the Maker Almighty—
Out of the infinite space of the Father—
Fluttered a soul on the wings of the morning,
Borne in the arms of the Angel of Birth.

Woven of dreams, and dream-child of the Father,
Light as a night thought and fading as swiftly—
Gone at a breath and yet strong in the passing—
Fluttered a soul on the wings of the noontide,
Borne in the arms of the Angel of Life.

Up through the silver and gray of the heavens,
Into the sleep of the Maker Almighty—
Into the infinite space of the Father—
Fluttered a soul on the wings of the evening,
Borne in the arms of the Angel of Death.
–Jill Douglas, age 13

PHANTOM SPRING

October came in lavender
This year, it seems to me;
In other years she wore burnt orange
And scarlet on each tree.

She stole the colors of the spring,
And put them in her hair;
She stole the very scent of spring
To April-ize the air!

She stole the freshness of spring rain,
She brought the April green,
She mixed it with the purple hues
That thrive when April's queen.

The grass sprang green within the yard,
Beside the warped-oak walk,
While by the house today I saw
An orchid four o'clock.

The lilacs, ever welcome,
Upon their twisted bough,
Purple framed in ashen grey,
Are frailly lovely now!

The figs are ripening purple
As they daily plumper grow,
While twilight makes an autumn sky
Seem mauve in sunset's glow.

Lantana on her brittle stem,
Beside the rain-bleached wall,
Nodded like an April thing
In the winds of fall.

And stranger yet, an iris bloomed
With light, chiffony face,
In violet, deep violet,
Down by the faucet's place.

It stood so dark, ethereal,
Upon an austere stalk,
It kept a solemn citadel
Beside the garden walk.

Perhaps it will not come again,
This eerie April thing;
But I shall not forget the year
We had a phantom spring.
–Bill Carnahan, age 15

There are certain points of technique that should be observed in the form of a poem. The margin line in all free verse poems and in poems rhyming in couplets should, in general, be even. None of the lines should be indented. Modern practice also allows all other forms to be written without indentations, although many poets prefer the indentations in rhymed verse. Indentation has only one purpose: to indicate lines that rhyme with each other. Where indentations are used, lines that rhyme with each other have the same margin line, as in the following:

BROOKLET

It skims along the pebbles,
   It races over rocks,
Just like a million fairies
   Tuning up busy clocks.
–Barbara Holmes, age 13

The following rules also should be observed:

1. Avoid trite rhymes, such as *love* and *above, trees* and *breeze, sing* and *spring.*
2. Except in a tercet, do not have more than two successive lines rhyming.
3. Rhymes should not be more than two lines apart.
4. Avoid near rhymes, such as *home* and *alone,* and rhymes identical in sound, such as *see* and *sea.*
5. Do not use the same rhyme word more than once in a short poem, unless the poem has a refrain.
6. Do not use forced rhymes, twisting words out of their

meaning for the sake of rhyme or saying things awkwardly in order to make the rhyme come out right.

Of course, professional poets break these rules from time to time, in order to achieve special effects; but beginners are not ready to experiment with prosody. They should be encouraged to follow the simple rules that will help to give their expressions the form of poetry; otherwise, their experiments may sound like a jumble of ignorance.

The rules, however, are not to be strictly applied to everything a child writes. The teacher must use them judiciously to help the older child who wishes to improve his poem.

The danger in teaching children to make rhymes is that they may concentrate on the rhyme to the detriment of the idea. For this reason it is wise to teach them first to write out their ideas in free verse form, to find the exact words to express their ideas, and then to try to put them into a special form without sacrificing the thought or the image.

8 Evaluating the Poetry of Children

FREE

A wild hawk caged,
  Beating against the bars,
Yearning for open spaces,
  Wanting the stars:

This was my spirit,
  Needing a friend to show
That the door was open,
  That I was free to go.
    –Ben Cramer, age 16

WHEN IS A POEM REALLY A *POEM?* What makes it a poem? What standards of evaluation shall we use in judging the work of children?

First of all, we must be willing to let the child's verse stand or fall (as poetry) on its own merits, to view it and criticize it dispassionately as a creative expression, avoiding sentimentality, overpraise, exploitation, and fussing over cleverness or cuteness. We must refrain from using the overzealous helping hand to add helpful words which will change or extend the idea so that the poem is no longer the child's own, checking firmly any tendency in ourselves to push or prod the child into making something we can show. We must remember that we have no personal stake in his poetry and that emphasis should be placed upon individual growth rather than upon the finished product.

In the process of learning to view a child's work objectively, without prejudice, without favor, and without attempting to read into it a reflection of our own emotional states, we must also avoid being fooled by cleverness or imitation. To make our judgments valid, we must know the age of the young writer and something about his maturity, background, experiences, and inhibitions. What is good poetry from a child of ten may be too immature and unthinking from a child of fifteen. An expression that is unsatisfactory from a child of good background and wide experience may be excellent from an underprivileged child or a child of meager background and limited experience. A piece of writing in which a stranger sees no value may show, by comparison with a child's earlier work, or in the light of our knowledge of his background and experience, the very sort of individual growth for which we are striving.

STANDARDS OF EVALUATION

Naturally, we shall not expect children's work to have all the qualities and characteristics that distinguish good adult poetry from mere verse; but if we know what those qualities are, we shall be better able to develop standards suitable to the age and grade of the children. Here is a brief summary of the essential qualities of poetry:

1. *Imagination.* Without imagination there is only cleverness and consequently only verse, not poetry. Imagination is shown in the conscious or unconscious use of imagery, analogy, figure of speech, and original thought and phrasing.
2. *Emotion.* Emotion is the fundamental basis, the motivating force of all poetry. When we read poetry, we seek a reflection of our own emotional experiences; when we write it, we attempt to share our emotional experiences with others.

3. *Idea.* Poetry contributes to literature either a new idea or a new approach to an old idea. It defines or implies a philosophy of life, interprets experience, or presents new insights. It adds something to the sum total of human wisdom, understanding, and appreciation.
4. *Universality.* If a poem presents an emotion or an experience that is or can be shared by the reader, it has universality, and its appeal is not limited to one class or race or period of time.
5. *Unity.* A poem should have unity of idea, of impression, and of treatment. It should have a central idea expressed in a single point of view with a single emotional effect. Both consistency and appropriateness in verse form and in rhythm help to contribute to the unity that is an important factor in producing the impact we expect of a poem.
6. *Rhythm.* Rhythm, whether patterned or cadenced, is essential to poetry. Without rhythm we have no poetry.
7. *Concreteness.* In order to communicate both his emotional reactions to experience and his insights, a poet must express his ideas in concrete terms that have sensuous appeals. He must make use of words that have picture quality, of figures of speech, and of comparisons that relate the unknown to the familiar.
8. *Pattern.* One thing that distinguishes poetry from all other forms of literature is pattern. The page patterns, the line and stanza patterns, the word patterns, the rhythm patterns, and the sound patterns all contribute to the artistic effect of the poems as well as to their impact and intensity.
9. *Intensity.* Intensity of emotional response to experience, intensity of imagination, and intensity of rhythm help to distinguish poetry from prose. Such intensity is produced, in part, by condensation of idea and phrasing; by the conscious and deliberate use of words with emotional associations; by an increased use of metaphor; by emphasis on the interpretation of experience in terms of the five senses; and by expression not in terms of logic and reason, but in terms of emotional reaction and spiritual intuition.
10. *Artistic Significance* (Impact). Artistic significance includes and transcends the other qualities of poetry. A poem has artistic significance if in form, in emotion, in idea it makes a significant contribution to our culture. Writing which is merely imitative lacks such significance. Poetry which has

artistic significance is original, displays awareness and insight, and bears the stamp of the author's personality.

In evaluating the poetry of a child, we must look first at the content and ask ourselves if the poet has anything to say and if he has said it effectively. Next, we must examine his intention and decide whether his purpose is to express himself or to please the teacher and seek praise. Finally, we must examine form and technique. Although our standard of values must be flexible and must be adapted to the age and grade of the child or the group, there are certain specific things we can look for that will help us in our evaluation. The following summary lists them:

1. *Originality*. Poems by children of any age should show originality of thought or phrasing or both, as well as originality in the choice of words and in the way words are put together.
2. *Sincerity*. A poem is sincere if it says what the author really thinks and feels. It is not sincere if the author is trying to be clever or facetious or to ape an adult writing down to children.
3. *Imagery*. The imagery or picture quality in a child's poem shows imagination at work to produce at least simple analogies and picturesque details. The imagery should not be imitative, but new and fresh.
4. *Idea*. If a child presents a new thought or a new image, or expresses an old idea in new terms, or exhibits originality of phrasing, he is making an intellectual contribution to poetry. His poem is of value if he honestly expresses in his own way an idea new to him, even though it is not new to the world.
5. *Feeling*. Children can be taught that a poem into which the poet puts some of his own feeling is of greater value than the poem that merely paints a pretty picture. We cannot expect them to show the depth of emotional power and awareness evident in adult poetry; but we can expect sincerity of feeling.
6. *Universality*. If children write about experiences or feelings that are or can be shared by other children of their own age, their poems have universality.
7. *Unity*. Children can be taught that a poem, like a paragraph,

should be about one subject, should maintain one point of view throughout, and should not mix rhythms and patterns.

8. *Rhythm.* Rhythm in the poetry of children may be simple, but there must be some sort of rhythm, either patterned or cadenced, if the poems are to have poetic significance. Chopped-up prose will not do. Free verse must be cadenced, and the cadences must be recognizable when read aloud.
9. *Accuracy.* Accuracy in the use of words is taken for granted in the poetry of adults, but must be listed as a qualification of good poetry by children. A poem should be grammatically correct, should use words accurately and consistently, and should avoid clichés, inversions, contractions, and poeticisms. It must be intelligible.
10. *Artistic Significance.* A child's work has artistic significance if it shows originality, an awareness of truth or beauty or significance, an attempt at patterning, and sincerity of feeling.

If a child's poem has even one of the characteristics of poetry as outlined, it indicates the poetic spirit at work, and it should be saved. It may be a scrawled sentence or two, poorly spelled, with no attempt at line division; but if the spark of originality is there, one should fan it and offer the kind of encouragement that will enable the child to select the original bit and build a real poem around it.

EVALUATIONS

Rules are not of much value unless they work. In the following pages we shall attempt to apply our standards of evaluation to specific poems that were selected for publication. Each poem has been chosen because it is outstanding in at least one particular.

RAINBOW SHADOW

A rainbow looks like two
With its shadow
In the water.
—*Viola Phillips, age 7*

1. *Originality.* This poem has originality of thought and phrasing. "Looks like two" is fresh.
2. *Imagery.* Picturesqueness is evident in the idea of the rainbow reflected in the water.
3. *Idea.* The connection of the rainbow with its shadow offers a new approach.
4. *Feeling.* The child is too young to make the emotional approach; but there is sincerity in the expression of thought, and perhaps there is a little feeling of wonder at the rainbow.
5. *Universality.* Seeing the rainbow and finding another in the water is a common childhood experience.
6. *Unity.* There is only one subject and one point of view.
7. *Rhythm.* There is almost a singing quality to the short cadences.
8. *Accuracy.* The use of words is entirely satisfactory. There is no triteness, nor is there ambiguity or vagueness.
9. *Artistic Significance.* The poem shows an awareness of beauty in nature and of a scientific truth, that reflections double things.

DEWDROPS

Little dewdrops on the vine,
I like to watch your diamonds shine;
Little star-lights up so high,
Are you the dewdrops of the sky?
—*Jimmie Davis, age 9*

The outstanding qualities of this poem are the rhythm, the parallel patterning of thought, and the imagination evident in the last line. "Dewdrops of the sky" shows originality of phrasing. And there is sincerity of feeling in the poem, which sounds like a child and has the child's point of view.

SONG

A little bird
Hopped on my window.
His song
Got into my dream.
—*June Nakagiri, age 6*

In this poem the outstanding quality is originality of phrasing. "His song got into my dream" is delightfully fresh and is an imaginative way of expressing a rather common experience. The poem is sincere; it sounds like a child's natural way of expression. It has a definite, cadenced rhythm.

STOKOWSKI'S HANDS

Hands smoothly glide on the air.
Quiet music, now they say.
Softly it dies like a whisper,
Creeping across the minds of players
Like drifting twilight shadows.
His hands move to and fro,
Up, down, like water over rocks,
Now sedately gliding.
Cymbals crash! Quiet, men.
Then hands glide . . . the end.
–*Constance Johnston, age 12*

1. *Originality.* The idea is original. How many people attending a concert would write about the conductor's *hands?* The phrasing is original, accurate, and vivid.
2. *Imagery.* The third, fifth, and seventh lines contain excellent images.
3. *Idea.* There is intellectual contribution in the idea of the close relationship between the conductor's hands, the music and the audience. This is an interpretation of experience in the terms of emotion.
4. *Feeling.* The poem makes strong emotional appeal. The reader is carried along with the author to the crashing climax.
5. *Universality.* Many of us have had and all of us could have similar experiences.
6. *Unity.* The poem is about one subject—Stokowski's hands—and maintains one point of view.
7. *Rhythm.* Although it is written in free verse, the poem is full of musical cadences.
8. *Accuracy.* The author has made excellent use of exact and significant wording. There is no triteness, and there is no imitation.

9. *Artistic Significance.* This poem has a definite contribution to make. It gives us a new point of view on a concert. It points out relationships and gives us the feeling of having shared with the author a new and thrilling experience. It stands on its own merits as a poem.

BACKGROUNDS

Shadows are not sad:
They are just backgrounds
For beauty.
–Ellen Preston, age 12

The chief characteristic of this poem is an idea which is new because it contradicts a generally accepted notion, although we immediately recognize the truth when it is pointed out to us. Here the poet is the interpreter.

This is a poem of idea rather than of imagery, but it has originality and universality. The only emotion expressed is a sober sincerity; but each reader interprets the poem in the light of his own experience with shadows or the shadow idea, and therefore the poem has emotional appeal.

LAUGHTER

The sea
Is like a cry
Of laughter.
–Dorothy Ashley, age 12

The originality of the imagery and its fortuitous expression, together with marked cadence, give significance to this poem.

DIVIDED ROAD

I was walking along a road one day
When I came to a river
That ran across it.
As I watched it flow, I thought:
The road of life
Has a river flowing across it.
On one side of the river
Is the land of the living.
On the other side
Is the land of the dead.
I sometimes wonder which is the most happy,
The home of the living,
Or the home of the dead.
–Elroy Duran, age 11

The principal merit in this poem lies in the thought and in the way in which it is expressed. The imagery is original. The strong emotional appeal depends for its effect upon the experience of the reader. The poem makes an original contribution because it shows a new way of expressing an old idea.

DYING SUN

A dying ember was the sun;
I watched in growing wonder
Until upon the field of night
The sky was torn asunder.
Still gazing at the evening sky,
I saw the tiny starlets bloom,
Like teardrops; for the sun they cry.
They drift into an unlit room.
–Sydney DeVore, age 15

Here we have a new way of looking at the sunset, and a very original way. There is something in this poem that approaches the mystical. It was chosen for publication because of this suggestion of mysticism, because of the excellent imagery, and because of the rhythm and the originality of the phrasing.

EGYPT

Oh, the land of Egypt,
The child of Father Nile,
Is like an exotic woman
Clothed in a cloud of mystery,
Before mystic shrines
With incense burning.
I can still see the priests of Ra
Walking among the ruins
On a moonlight evening.
–Virginia Wheatley, age 12

The emotional appeal in "Egypt" is the romance of a far-off place. There is an excellent image in the first three lines. The word choice is good. The poet has made a new approach to an old idea, preserving and heightening the romance and mystery of an ancient time. The rhythm moves by satisfactory cadences, and the total effect of the poem is pleasing.

ON THE RIVER

The junks bob up and down
With the lazy sway of that yellow water.
But there is a breeze,
And it carries the mellow smell
Of rice to be served in pottery.
–Don Evans, age 15

Through the use of picturesque detail, the poet has recreated the oriental atmosphere. His ability to reproduce a picture in words shows creative imagination at work. The free-verse rhythm, strongly marked, helps out the picture. The poem is an appreciation rather than an intellectual contribution. Its emotional appeal lies in its power to call up in one who has lived in China a feeling of nostalgia.

CUPS OF GOLD

Jonquils are cups of gold.
They droop their heads so low,
I think that all the gold they have
Will spill.
–Dorothy Marrick, age 13

The value in this poem lies almost entirely in the imagery and the simple and direct expression of the image. The lines are musical when read aloud, and the phrasing is original.

The foregoing illustrations are intended to demonstrate a method of evaluating the poems of children by looking for merits rather than for flaws. Small flaws, if pounced upon first, sometimes hide large values. After we have found the values, the flaws will not loom so large.

Bibliography

BOOKS ABOUT POETRY APPRECIATION AND POETRY WRITING

Abercrombie, Lascelles, *Poetry: Its Music and Meaning.* London: Oxford University Press, 1932.

Abercrombie, Lascelles, *The Theory of Poetry.* New York: Harcourt, Brace & World, Inc., 1926.

Abney, Louise, and Grace Rowe, *Choral Speaking Arrangements for the Lower Grades.* Boston: Expression Company, 1937.

Abney, Louise, *Choral Speaking Arrangements for the Upper Grades.* Boston: Expression Company, 1937.

Alden, Raymond, *Introduction to Poetry.* New York: Holt, Rinehart and Winston, Inc., 1909.

Arnstein, Flora J., *Adventures into Poetry.* Stanford, California: Stanford University Press, 1951.

Auslander, Joseph, and Frank Ernest Hill, *The Winged Horse.* New York: Doubleday & Company, 1927.

Austin, Mary, *The American Rhythm.* Boston: Houghton Mifflin Company, 1930.

Bailey, Ruth, *A Dialogue on Modern Poetry.* London: Oxford University Press, 1939.

Barfield, Owen, *Poetic Diction.* London: Faber and Gwyer, 1928.

Barnes, Walter, *The Children's Poets.* New York: Harcourt, Brace & World, Inc., 1924.

Baum, P. F., *Principles of English Versification.* Cambridge, Massachusetts: Harvard University Press, 1922.

Beach, Joseph Warren, *A Romantic View of Poetry.* Minneapolis: University of Minnesota Press, 1944.

Blyth, R. H., *Haiku,* in four volumes. Tokyo: Hokuseido, 1950.

Bradley, G. F., *About English Poetry.* London: Oxford University Press, 1929.

Brooks, Cleanth, *Modern Poetry and the Tradition.* Chapel Hill, North Carolina: University of North Carolina Press, 1939.

Brooks, Cleanth, *The Well Wrought Urn.* New York: Harcourt, Brace & World, Inc., 1947.

Brooks, Cleanth, and Robert Penn Warren, *Understanding Poetry.* New York: Holt, Rinehart and Winston, Inc., 1950.

Brown, Rollo Walter, *The Creative Spirit.* New York: Harper & Brothers, 1925.

Buell, Robert K., *Verse Writing Simplified.* Stanford, California: Stanford University Press, 1940.

Cane, Melville, *Making a Poem.* New York: Harcourt, Brace & World, Inc., 1953.

Carruth, William Herbert, *Verse Writing.* New York: The Macmillan Company, 1917.

Chapin, Elsa, and Thomas Russell, *A New Approach to Poetry.* Chicago: University of Chicago Press, 1929.

Conrad, Lawrence H., *Teaching Creative Writing.* New York: Appleton-Century-Crofts, Inc., 1937.

Cooper, Charles W., *Preface to Poetry.* New York: Harcourt, Brace & World, Inc., 1946.

Crum, Ralph B., *Scientific Thought in Poetry.* New York: Columbia University Press, 1931.

Dalgliesh, Alice, *First Experiences with Literature.* New York: Charles Scribner's Sons, 1937.

Daniels, Earl R. K., *The Art of Reading Poetry.* New York: Holt, Rinehart and Winston, Inc., 1949.

Day-Lewis, Cecil, *Enjoying Poetry.* London: Cambridge University Press, 1959.

Day-Lewis, Cecil, *A Hope for Poetry.* Oxford: Basil Blackwell & Mott, Ltd., 1934.

Day-Lewis, Cecil, *The Poetic Image.* New York: Oxford University Press, 1947.

Day-Lewis, Cecil, *Poetry for You.* Oxford: Basil Blackwell & Mott, Ltd., 1945.

Day-Lewis, Cecil, *The Poet's Way of Knowledge.* England: Cambridge University Press, 1959.

Deering, Mrs. Ivah Everett, *The Creative Home.* New York: Richard R. Smith, Publisher, Inc., 1930.

De Selincourt, Aubrey, *On Reading Poetry.* Denver, Colorado: Alan Swallow, Publisher, 1952.

Deutsch, Babette, *Poetry Handbook.* New York: Funk and Wagnalls Company, 1957.

Deutsch, Babette, *Poetry in Our Time.* New York: Holt, Rinehart and Winston, Inc., 1952.

Deutsch, Babette, *Potable Gold.* New York: W. W. Norton & Company, Inc., 1929.

Deutsch, Babette, *This Modern Poetry.* New York: W. W. Norton & Company, Inc., 1935.

Doubleday, Neal Frank, *Studies in Poetry.* New York: Harper and Brothers, 1949.

Downey, June E., *Creative Imagination.* New York: Harcourt, Brace & World, Inc., 1929.

Drew, Elizabeth A., *Discovering Poetry.* New York: W. W. Norton & Company, Inc., 1933.

Drew, Elizabeth A., *Poetry: A Modern Guide.* New York: W. W. Norton & Company, Inc., 1959.

Drew, Elizabeth A., and J. L. Sweeney, *Directions in Modern Poetry.* New York: W. W. Norton & Company, Inc., 1940.

Drinkwater, John, *The Way of Poetry.* London: William Collins Sons & Co., Ltd., 1930.

Eastman, Max, *The Enjoyment of Poetry, with Anthology.* New York: Charles Scribner's Sons, 1951.

Eliot, T. S., *The Three Voices of Poetry.* London: Cambridge University Press, 1954.

Empson, William, *Seven Types of Ambiguity.* New York: New Directions, 1947.

Erskine, John, *The Kinds of Poetry and Other Essays.* Indianapolis: The Bobbs-Merrill Company, Inc., 1930.

Farren, Robert, *How to Enjoy Poetry.* New York: Sheed and Ward, Inc., 1948.

Fogerty, Elsie, *The Speaking of English Verse.* London: J. M. Dent & Sons, Ltd., 1923.

Frankenberg, Lloyd, *Pleasure Dome.* Boston: Houghton Mifflin Company, 1949.

Frawley, Honora M., *Certain Procedures of Studying Poetry in the Fifth Grade.* New York: Teachers' College, Columbia University, 1932.

Garrod, Heathcote W., *The Profession of Poetry.* Oxford: Clarendon Press, 1929.

Gilchrist, Marie E., *Writing Poetry.* Boston: Houghton Mifflin Company, 1932.

Gullan, Marjorie, *Poetry Speaking for Children.* London: Methuen & Co., Ltd., 1939.
Gullan, Marjorie, *Spoken Poetry in the Schools.* London: Methuen & Co., Ltd., 1930.
Gurrey, Percival, *The Appreciation of Poetry.* London: Oxford University Press, 1935.
Hall, Howard Judson, *Types of Poetry.* Boston: Ginn & Company, 1931.
Harris, L. S., *The Nature of English Poetry.* London: J. M. Dent & Sons, Ltd., 1931.
Henderson, Harold Gould, *The Bamboo Room.* Boston: Houghton Mifflin Company, 1934.
Highet, Gilbert, *Powers of Poetry.* New York: Oxford University Press, 1960.
Hillyer, Robert, *First Principles of Verse.* Boston: *Writer,* 1950.
Holmes, John, *Writing Poetry.* Boston: *Writer,* 1960.
Hooper, John, *Poetry in the New Curriculum.* Brattleboro, Vermont: Stephen Daye Press, 1932.
Hourd, Marjorie L., *The Education of the Poetic Spirit.* London: William Heinemann, Ltd., 1949.
Housman, A. E., *The Name and Nature of Poetry.* New York: The Macmillan Company, 1933.
Hubbell, Jay B., and John O. Beaty, *An Introduction to Poetry.* New York: The Macmillan Company, 1936.
Huber, Miriam Blanton, *Children's Interests in Poetry.* New York: Rand McNally & Company, 1927.
Hughes, Glenn, *Imagism and the Imagists.* London: Oxford University Press, 1931.
Jones, Llewellyn, *First Impressions.* New York: Alfred A. Knopf, Inc., 1925.
Kelly, William Roswell, Helen M. Brogan, and Donald F. Connors, *Poetry in the Classroom.* New York: William H. Sadlier, Inc., 1940.
Kenner, Hugh, *The Art of Poetry.* New York: Holt, Rinehart and Winston, Inc., 1959.
Keppie, Elizabeth, *The Teaching of Choric Speech.* Boston: Expression Company, (no date listed).
Kilby, Clyde S., *Poetry and Life.* New York: The Odyssey Press, Inc., 1953.

Kirk, Richard R., and Roger McCutcheon, *Introduction to the Study of Poetry.* New York: American Book Company, 1934.

Korg, Jacob, *Introduction to Poetry.* New York: Holt, Rinehart and Winston, Inc., 1959.

Kreuzer, James R., *Elements of Poetry.* New York: The Macmillan Company, 1955.

Kreymborg, Alfred, *Our Singing Strength.* New York: Coward-McCann, Inc., 1929.

Lanier, Sydney, *The Science of English Verse.* New York: Charles Scribner's Sons, 1908.

Leavis, Frank R., *New Bearings in English Poetry.* London: Chatto & Windus, 1954.

Lewis, Benjamin, *Creative Poetry.* Stanford, California: Stanford University Press, 1931.

Long, Mason, *Poetry and Its Forms.* New York: G. P. Putnam's Sons, 1938.

Lowell, Amy, *Poetry and Poets.* Boston: Houghton Mifflin Company, 1930.

Lowell, Amy, *Tendencies in Modern American Poetry.* New York: The Macmillan Company, 1917.

Lowes, John L., *Convention and Revolt in Poetry.* Boston: Houghton Mifflin Company, 1919.

Mackail, J. W., *Lectures on Poetry.* New York: Longmans, Green & Co., Inc., 1914.

MacLeish, Archibald, *Poetry and Experience.* Boston: Houghton Mifflin Company, 1960.

MacNeice, Louis, *Modern Poetry.* New York: Oxford University Press, 1938.

Mansfield, Margery, *Workers in Fire.* New York: Longmans, Green & Co., Inc., 1937.

Matthews, Brander, *A Study of Versification.* Boston: Houghton Mifflin Company, 1911.

Mearns, Hughes, *The Creative Adult.* New York: Doubleday & Company, Inc., 1940.

Mearns, Hughes, *Creative Power.* New York: Doubleday & Company, Inc., 1929.

Mearns, Hughes, *Creative Youth.* New York: Doubleday & Company, Inc., 1925.

Miller, H. Augustus, Jr., *Creative Writing of Verse.* New York: American Book Company, 1932.

Miller, Harry Lloyd, *Creative Learning and Teaching.* New York: Charles Scribner's Sons, 1927.

Millett, Fred, *Reading Poetry.* New York: Harper & Brothers, 1950.

Moore, Marianne, *Predilections.* New York: The Viking Press, 1955.

Neihardt, John G., *Poetic Values and Our Need of Them.* New York: The Macmillan Company, 1925.

Neilson, William A., *Essentials of Poetry.* Boston: Houghton Mifflin Company, 1912.

Osgood, Charles G., *Poetry as a Means of Grace.* New York: Oxford University Press, 1941.

Parrish, Wayland, *Reading Aloud.* New York: Thomas Nelson & Sons, 1932.

Perrine, Lawrence, *Sound and Sense.* New York: Harcourt, Brace & World, Inc., 1956.

Perry, Bliss, *A Study of Poetry.* Boston: Houghton Mifflin Company, 1920.

Prescott, Frederick Clarke, *The Poetic Mind.* New York: The Macmillan Company, 1922.

Ransom, John Crowe, *The World's Body.* New York: Charles Scribner's Sons, 1938.

Read, Herbert, *Form in Modern Poetry.* London: Sheed and Ward, Ltd., 1932.

Richards, I. A., *Practical Criticism.* New York: Harcourt, Brace and World, Inc., 1929.

Richards, I. A., *Science and Poetry.* London: Routledge and Kegan Paul, Ltd., 1935.

Ridley, Maurice Roy, *Poetry and the Ordinary Reader.* New York: E. P. Dutton & Co., 1939.

Rylands, George H., *Words and Poetry.* New York: Payson and Clark, 1928.

Sanblom, Mrs. Lola, *Every Child and Poetry Rhythm.* Glendale, California: Author Publisher, 1938.

Sanders, DeWitt, *A Poetry Primer.* New York: Holt, Rinehart and Winston, Inc., 1935.

Santayana, George, *Interpretations of Poetry and Religion.* New York: Charles Scribner's Sons, 1900.

Sapir, Edward, *Language.* New York: Harcourt, Brace & World, Inc., 1921.

Savage, D. S., *The Personal Principle: Studies in Modern Poetry.* London: Routledge & Kegan Paul, Ltd., 1944.
Scarfe, Francis, *Auden and After.* London: Routledge & Kegan Paul, Ltd., 1942.
Seely, Howard F., *Enjoying Poetry in School.* New York: Johnson Publishing Company, 1931.
Simon, Charlie May, *Lays of the New Land.* New York: E. P. Dutton & Co., 1946.
Skelton, Robin, *The Poetic Pattern.* Berkeley, California: University of California Press, 1956.
Smith, Chard Powers, *Pattern and Variation in Poetry.* New York: Charles Scribner's Sons, 1932.
Spender, Stephen, *The Creative Element.* London: Hamish Hamilton, 1953.
Stageberg, Norman C., and W. L. Anderson, *Poetry as Experience.* New York: American Book Company, 1952.
Stauffer, Donald, *The Nature of Poetry.* New York: W. W. Norton & Co., Inc., 1946.
Sussams, T., *Poetry and the Teacher.* London: Nelson, Publishers, 1949.
Tate, Allen, *On the Limits of Poetry.* Denver, Colorado: Alan Swallow, 1948.
Tillyard, E. M. W., *Poetry Direct and Oblique.* New York: The Macmillan Company, 1945.
Trevelyan, Robert C., *Thamyris.* New York: E. P. Dutton & Co., 1925.
Untermeyer, Louis, *Doorways to Poetry.* New York: Harcourt, Brace & World, Inc., 1938.
Untermeyer, Louis, *The Forms of Poetry.* New York: Harcourt, Brace & World, Inc., 1926.
Untermeyer, Louis, *Modern American and Modern British Poetry,* Mid-Century Edition. New York: Harcourt, Brace & World, Inc., 1950.
Untermeyer, Louis, and Carter Davidson, *Poetry: Its Appreciation and Enjoyment.* New York: Harcourt, Brace & World, Inc., 1934.
Wells, Henry W., *The American Way of Poetry.* New York: Columbia University Press, 1943.
Wells, Henry W., *New Poets from Old.* New York: Columbia University Press, 1940.

Wells, Henry W., *Where Poetry Stands Now.* Toronto: Ryerson Press, 1948.

Wilder, A. N., *Modern Poetry and the Christian Tradition.* New York: Charles Scribner's Sons, 1952.

Wilder, A. N., *The Spiritual Aspects of the New Poetry.* New York: Harper & Brothers, 1940.

Wilkinson, Bonaro, *The Poetic Way of Release.* New York: Alfred A. Knopf, 1932.

Wilkinson, Marguerite, *New Voices.* New York: The Macmillan Company, 1928.

Wilkinson, Marguerite, *The Way of the Makers.* New York: The Macmillan Company, 1925.

Williams, Charles, *Reason and Beauty in the Poetic Mind.* Oxford: Clarendon Press, 1933.

Wilson, Katherine M., *The Real Rhythm in English Poetry.* London: Jonathan Cape, Ltd., 1929.

Wilson, Katharine M., *Sound and Meaning in English Poetry.* London: Jonathan Cape, Ltd., 1930.

Wood, Clement, *The Art and Technique of Writing Poetry.* New York: Greenberg: Publisher, Inc., 1940.

Wood, Clement, *The Craft of Poetry.* New York: E. P. Dutton & Co., 1929.

Wrinn, Mary J. J., *The Hollow Reed.* New York: Harper & Brothers, 1935.

Zillman, Lawrence, *The Elements of English Verse.* New York: The Macmillan Company, 1935.

Zillman, Lawrence, *Writing Your Poem.* New York: Funk & Wagnalls Company, 1950.

ANTHOLOGIES OF POETRY FOR CHILDREN AND YOUNG PEOPLE

	AGES
Adams, Florence, and Elizabeth McCarrick, *Highways and Holidays.* New York: E. P. Dutton & Co., 1927.	4–9
Adshead, Gladys, and Annis Duff, *An Inheritance of Poetry.* Boston: Houghton Mifflin Company, 1948.	6–16
Aldis, Dorothy, *All Together.* New York: G. P. Putnam's Sons, 1952.	4–8
Arbuthnot, May Hill, *Time for Poetry.* New York: Scott, Foresman and Company, 1952.	6–12
Association for Childhood Education, *Sung Under the Silver Umbrella.* New York: The Macmillan Company, 1943.	3–8
Auslander, Joseph, and Frank Ernest Hill, *The Winged Horse.* New York: Doubleday & Company, Inc., 1927.	7–16
Austin, Mary, *Children Sing in the Far West.* Boston: Houghton Mifflin Company, 1928.	6–12
Barrows, Marjorie, *One Hundred Best Poems for Boys and Girls.* Chicago: Albert Whitman & Company, 1930.	6–12
Bates, Herbert, *Modern Lyric Poetry.* Evanston, Illinois: Row, Peterson and Company, 1929.	12–18
Behn, Harry, *The House Beyond the Hill.* New York: Pantheon Books, Inc., 1955.	6–10
Behn, Harry, *The Little Hill.* New York: Harcourt, Brace & World, Inc., 1949.	6–9
Behn, Harry, *Windy Morning.* New York: Harcourt, Brace & World, Inc., 1953.	2–4
Benét, William Rose, and Conrad Aiken, *An Anthology of Famous English and American Poetry.* New York: Modern Library, Inc., 1945.	12–18
Benét, William Rose, *Poems for Youth.* New York: E. P. Dutton & Co., 1925.	6–12

Benét, William Rose, and Norman Cousins, *The Poetry of Freedom*. New York: Random House, Inc., 1945. 9–18

Benét, William Rose, *With Wings as Eagles*. New York: Dodd, Mead and Co., 1940. 8–18

Blanding, Don, *Vagabond House*. New York: Dodd, Mead & Company, Inc., 1928. 12 up

Bontemps, Arna W., *Golden Slippers*. New York: Harper & Brothers, 1941. 7–12

Brewton, John E., *Gaily We Parade*. New York: The Macmillan Company, 1940. 6–12

Brewton, John E., *Under the Tent of the Sky*. New York: The Macmillan Company, 1937. 3–8

Brewton, Sara W., and John E. Brewton, *Bridled with Rainbows*. New York: The Macmillan Company, 1949. 4–8

Brewton, Sara W., and John E. Brewton, *Christmas Bells Are Ringing*. New York: The Macmillan Company, 1951. 4–9

Brown, Margaret Wise, *Nibble, Nibble*. New York: William R. Scott, Inc., 1959. 5–8

Bynner, Witter, *The Jade Mountain*. New York: Alfred A. Knopf, 1929. 8–14

Carhart, George S., and Paul A. McGlee, *Magic Casements*. New York: The Macmillan Company, 1926. 5–12

Clark, Frances E., *Poetry's Plea for Animals*. New York: Lothrop, Lee & Shepard Co., Inc., 1927. 6–12

Coatsworth, Elizabeth, *Poems*. New York: The Macmillan Company, 1957. 6–12

Coatsworth, Elizabeth, *Summer Grow*. New York: The Macmillan Company, 1948. 4–7

Cook, Howard W., *Our Poets of Today*. New York: Dodd, Mead and Co., 1926. 12–16

Cooper, Alice, *Poems of Today*. Boston: Ginn & Company, 1924. 9–16

Daringer, Helen F., and Anne T. Eaton, *The Poet's Craft*. New York: Harcourt, Brace & World Inc., 1935. 9–16

Davis, M. G., *Girls' Book of Verse*. Philadelphia: Frederick A. Stokes Company, 1922. 6–12

De La Mare, Walter, *Bells and Grass*. New York: The Viking Press, Inc., 1942. 5–12

De La Mare, Walter, *A Child's Day*. New York: Holt, Rinehart and Winston, Inc., 1923. 1–3

De La Mare, *Come Hither*. New York: Alfred A. Knopf, 1928. 6–12

De La Mare, Walter, *Peacock Pie*. E. M. Hale & Company, (no date). 4–8

De La Mare, Walter, *Poems for Children*. New York: Holt, Rinehart and Winston, Inc., 1930. 3–8

De La Mare, Walter, *Rhymes and Verse*. New York: Holt, Rinehart and Winston, Inc., 1947. 4–9

Dickinson, Emily, *Bolts of Melody*. New York: Harper & Brothers, 1945. 9 up

Dickinson, Emily, *Poems for Youth*. New York: Little Brown & Company, 1934. 6–12

Dickinson, Kate L., *Modern Lyrics*. New York: Allyn and Bacon, Inc., 1930. 12–18

Farjeon, Eleanor, *Cherrystones*. Philadelphia: J. B. Lippincott Company, 1944. 5–8

Farjeon, Eleanor, *The Children's Bells*. New York: Henry Z. Walck, Inc., 1960. 8–12

Farjeon, Eleanor, *Poems for Children*. Philadelphia: J. B. Lippincott Company, 1951. 4–6

Farjeon, Eleanor, *Sing for Your Supper*, Philadelphia: J. B. Lippincott Company, 1938. 8–12

Ferris, Helen J., *Favorite Poems Old and New*. New York: Doubleday & Company, Inc., 1957. 6–16

Field, Rachel L., *Branches Green*. New York: The Macmillan Company, 1934. 6–9

Field, Rachel, *Poems*. New York: The Macmillan Company, 1957. 6–16

Field, Rachel, *Taxis and Toadstools*. New York: Doubleday & Company, Inc., 1926. 7–10

Fish, Helen D., *Boys' Book of Verse*. Philadelphia: J. B. Lippincott Company, 1951. 5–9

French, Roy L., *Recent Poetry*. Boston: D. C. Heath and Company, 1926. 12–18

Frost, Frances, *The Little Whistler.* New York: Whittlesey House, 1949. 7–10
Frost, Robert, *Come In, and Other Poems.* New York: Holt, Rinehart and Winston, Inc., 1943. 9–16
Frost, Robert, *North of Boston.* New York: Holt, Rinehart and Winston, Inc., 1915. 12–18
Frost, Robert, *Road Not Taken.* New York: Holt, Rinehart and Winston, Inc., 1951. 7–16
Frost, Robert, *You Come, Too.* New York: Holt, Rinehart and Winston, Inc., 1959. 6–18
Fyleman, R., *Fairies.* New York: Doubleday & Company, Inc., 1920. 4–6
Geismer, Barbara P., and Antoinette B. Suter, *Very Young Verses.* Boston: Houghton Mifflin Company, 1945. 4–7
Gordon, Margery, and Marie King, *Verses of Our Day.* New York: Appleton-Century-Crofts, Inc., 1936. 7–12
Grahame, Kenneth, *Cambridge Book of Poetry for Children.* New York: G. P. Putnam's Sons, 1933. 9–12
Grover, Eulalie O., *My Caravan.* Chicago: Albert Whitman & Company, 1931. 4–12
Hallock, Grace Tabor, *Bird in the Bush.* New York: E. P. Dutton & Co., Inc., 1930. 6–12
Harrington, Mildred, *Ring-a-Round.* New York: The Macmillan Company, 1930. 3–8
Hazeltine, Alice J., and Eliza S. Smith, *The Year Around.* Nashville, Tennessee: Abingdon Press, 1956. 7–12
Headland, Isaac Taylor, *Chinese Mother Goose Rhymes.* Westwood, New Jersey: Fleming H. Revell Company, 1900. 6–12
Holland, Sargent, *Historic Poems and Ballads.* Philadelphia: Macrae Smith Co., 1912. 12–16
Housman, Alfred E., *A Shropshire Lad.* New York: Holt, Rinehart and Winston, Inc., 1924. 9–18
Huffard, Grace T., L. M. Carlisle, and H. J. Ferris, *My Poetry Book.* New York: Holt, Rinehart and Winston, Inc., 1956. 6–12
Hughes, Langston, *The Dreamkeeper.* New York: Alfred A. Knopf, 1932. 10–18
Hutchinson, V. S., *Chimney Corner Poems.* New York: G. P. Putnam's Sons, 1929. 1–6

Hutchinson, V. S., *Fireside Poems.* New York: G. P. Putnam's Sons, 1930. 3–6

Knippel, Dolores, *Poems for the Very Young Child.* Chicago: Albert Whitman & Company, 1932. 3–6

Kreymborg, Alfred, *An Anthology of American Poetry.* New York: Tudor Publishing Co., 1935. 12–18

Lieberman, Elias, *Poems for Enjoyment.* New York: Harper & Brothers, 1931. 12–18

Lindsay, Vachel, *Appleseed Johnny and Other Poems.* New York: The Macmillan Company, 1928. 4–9

Livingston, Myra Cohn, *Whispers and Other Poems.* New York: Harcourt, Brace & World, Inc., 1957. 5–9

Lowell, Amy, *Fir Flower Tablets.* Boston: Houghton Mifflin Company, 1924. 12–18

McDonald, Gerald, *A Way of Knowing.* New York: Thomas Y. Crowell Company, 1959. 12–18

McNeil, Horace J., and Clarence Stratton, *Poems for a Machine Age.* New York: McGraw-Hill Book Company, Inc., 1941. 9–18

Masefield, John, *Salt Water Poems and Ballads.* New York: The Macmillan Company, 1916. 6–16

Mikels, Rosa M., and Grace Shoup, *Poetry of Today.* New York: Charles Scribner's Sons, 1927. 12–18

Millay, Edna St. Vincent, *Mine the Harvest.* New York: Harper & Brothers, 1954. 10–18

Millay, Edna St. Vincent, *Poems Selected for Young People.* New York: Harper & Brothers, 1929. 6–12

Miller, Mary Britton, *Menagerie.* New York: The Macmillan Company, 1928. 6–12

Milne, A. A., *Now We Are Six.* New York: E. P. Dutton & Co., Inc., 1927. 1–4

Milne, A. A., *When We Were Very Young.* New York: E. P. Dutton & Co., Inc., 1924. 1–4

Monroe, Harriet, *The New Poetry.* New York: The Macmillan Company, 1932. 9–18

Palgrave, F. T., *Golden Treasury.* London: Oxford University Press, 1914. 12–18

Parker, Elinor M., *100 Poems about People.* New York: Thomas Y. Crowell Company, 1955. 11–16

Parker, Elinor M., *100 Story Poems.* New York: Thomas Y. Crowell Company, 1951. 5–9

Peterson, Isabel J., *The First Book of Poetry.* New York: Franklin Watts, Inc., 1954. 6–10

Plotz, Helen, *Imagination's Other Place.* New York: Thomas Y. Crowell Company, 1955. 12–18

Read, Herbert, *This Way, Delight.* New York: Pantheon Books, Inc., 1956. 6–18

Richards, Mrs. Waldo, *High Tide.* Boston: Houghton Mifflin Company, 1916. 12–18

Richards, Mrs. Waldo, *Magic Carpet.* Boston: Houghton Mifflin Company, 1924. 12–18

Richards, Mrs. Waldo, *Star-Points.* Boston: Houghton Mifflin Company, 1929. 12–18

Rittenhouse, J. B., *Little Book of American Poets.* Boston: Houghton Mifflin Company, 1929. 12–18

Rittenhouse, Jessie B., *Little Book of Modern Verse.* Boston: Houghton Mifflin Company, 1917. 9–18

Roberts, Elizabeth Madox, *Under the Tree.* New York: The Viking Press, 1930. 5–8

Rodman, B., *A New Anthology of Modern Poetry.* New York: Random House, Inc., 1938. 10–18

Rodman, Selden, *The Poetry of Flight.* New York: Duell, Sloan & Pearce, Inc., 1941. 9–18

Sandburg, Carl, *Early Moon.* New York: Harcourt, Brace & World, Inc., 1930. 5–12

Sechrist, Elizabeth, *One Thousand Poems for Children.* New York: Macrae Smith Co., 1946. 6–12

Shannon, Monica, *Goose Grass Rhymes.* New York: Doubleday & Co., Inc., 1930. 4–12

Stevenson, B. E., *The Home Book of Modern Verse.* New York: Holt, Rinehart and Winston, Inc., 1937. 6–18

Stevenson, B. E., *The Home Book of Verse for Young Folks.* New York: Holt, Rinehart and Winston, Inc., 1929. 3–16

Stevenson, B. E., *Poems of American History.* Boston: Houghton Mifflin Company, 1922. 9–18

Stevenson, Robert Louis, *A Child's Garden of Verses.* New York: Oxford University Press, 1947. 3–8

Swift, Hildegarde H., *North Star Shining.* New York: William Morrow & Company, Inc., 1947. 7–12
Teasdale, Sara, *Collected Poems.* New York: The Macmillan Company, 1937. 10–18
Teasdale, Sara, *Rainbow Gold.* New York: The Macmillan Company, 1922. 8–16
Teasdale, Sara, *Stars Tonight.* New York: The Macmillan Company, 1930. 8–12
Thompson, Blanche, *More Silver Pennies.* New York: The Macmillan Company, 1938. 3–9
Thompson, Blanche, *Silver Pennies.* New York: The Macmillan Company, 1925. 6–9
Thompson, Blanche, *With Harp and Flute.* New York: The Macmillan Company, 1935. 4–8
Thorn, Alice, *Singing Words.* New York: Charles Scribner's Sons, 1941. 3–4
Tietjens, Mrs. Eunice, *Poetry of the Orient.* New York: Alfred A. Knopf, 1928. 10–18
Untermeyer, Louis, *Book of Living Verse.* New York: Harcourt, Brace & World, Inc., 1932. 10–18
Untermeyer, Louis, *The Golden Treasury of Poetry.* New York: Golden Press, Inc., 1959. 6–16
Untermeyer, Louis, *Magic Circle.* New York: Harcourt, Brace & World, Inc., 1952. 6–9
Untermeyer, Louis, *Rainbow in the Sky.* New York: Harcourt, Brace & World, Inc., 1935. 3–8
Untermeyer, Louis, *Stars to Steer By.* New York: Harcourt, Brace & World, Inc., 1941. 5–10
Untermeyer, Louis, *This Singing World.* New York: Harcourt, Brace & World, Inc., 1923. 4–12
Untermeyer, Louis, *This Singing World for Younger Children.* New York: Harcourt, Brace & World, Inc., 1926. 4–12
Untermeyer, Louis, *A Treasury of Great Poems.* New York: Simon and Schuster, Inc., 1942. 9–18
Untermeyer, Louis, *Yesterday and Today.* New York: Harcourt, Brace & World, Inc., 1926. 5–10
Van Doren, Mark, *Anthology of World Poetry.* New York: Harcourt, Brace & World, Inc., 1936. 9–18

Van Doren, Mark, *Introduction to Poetry*. New York: Holt, Rinehart & Winston, Inc., 1951. 9–18

Van Doren, Mark, *Junior Anthology of World Poetry*. New York: Albert and Charles Boni, 1929. 6–12

Van Doren, Mark, *The World's Best Poems*. New York: Albert and Charles Boni, Inc., 1932. 12–18

Waley, Arthur, *A Hundred and Seventy Chinese Poems*. New York: Alfred A. Knopf, 1919. 12–18

Waley, Arthur, *Japanese Poetry*. Oxford: Clarendon Press, 1919. 12–18

Weiner, Jane, *Golden Book of Poetry*. New York: Simon and Schuster, Inc., 1947. K–4

Whitman, Walt, *I Hear the People Singing*. New York: International Publishers Co., Inc., 1946. 6–12

Wilkinson, Marguerite, *Contemporary Poetry*. New York: The Macmillan Company, 1923. 12–18

Williams, Oscar, *A Little Treasury of Modern Poetry*. New York: Charles Scribner's Sons, 1950. 9–18

Wylie, Elinor, *Collected Poems*. New York: Alfred A. Knopf, 1932. 10–18

Wynne, Annette, *For Days and Days*. Philadelphia: Frederick A. Stokes Company, 1919. 5–12

BOOKS CONTAINING POETRY BY CHILDREN AND YOUNG PEOPLE

Conkling, Hilda, *Poems by a Little Girl*. Philadelphia: Frederick A. Stokes Company, 1920.

Conkling, Hilda, *Shoes of the Wind*. New York: Frederick A. Stokes Company, 1922.

Conkling, Hilda, *Silverhorn*. New York: Frederick A. Stokes Company, 1924.

Crane, Nathalia, *The Janitor's Boy*. New York: Feltzer Publishing Co., 1924.

Crane, Nathalia, *Lava Lane and Other Poems*. New York: Feltzer Publishing Co., 1925.

Crane, Nathalia, *The Singing Crow and Other Poems*. New York: Albert and Charles Boni, Inc., 1926.

Gilchrist, Marie, *Writing Poetry*. Boston: Houghton Mifflin Company, 1932.

Mearns, Hughes, *Creative Youth*. New York: Doubleday & Company, Inc., 1925.
Miller, H. Augustus, Jr., *Creative Writing of Verse*. New York: American Book Company, 1932.
Mountsier, Mabel, *Singing Youth*. New York: Harper & Brothers, 1927.
Seeds, Corinne, *Childhood Expressions*. Cambridge: Cambridge University Press, 1931.
Wrinn, Mary J. J., *The Hollow Reed*. New York: Harper & Brothers, 1935.

INDEXES OF POETRY

Brewton, John E., and Sara W., *Index to Children's Poetry*. New York: H. W. Wilson Company, 1942.
Bruncken, H., *Subject Index to Poetry*. Chicago: American Library Association, 1940.
Dixon, R. J. (Ed.), *Granger's Index to Poetry*. New York: Columbia University Press, 1957.
Hastings, Henry C., *Spoken Poetry on Records and Tapes*. Chicago: American Library Association, 1957.
MacPherson, Maud R., *Children's Poetry Index*. New York: F. W. Faxon, Inc., 1928.
Sell, Violet, et al., *Subject Index to Poetry for Children and Young People*. Chicago: American Library Association, 1957.

Index

AUTHORS

TOPICS